NINJA™

BREAKTHROUGH BLENDING!

CREATIVE & DELICIOUS RECIPES
FOR YOUR NINJA™ BLENDER

Pascoe Publishing, Inc.
Rocklin, California

Cover & Interior Design by KB Designs
Published in the United States of America by

Pascoe Publishing, Inc.
Rocklin, California
www. pascoepublishing. com

ISBN: 978-1-929862-84-9

Printed in China

TABLE OF CONTENTS

INTRODUCTION

In a world filled with new styles of eating, new foods and food products, and new appliances in which to prep and cook those foods, it would be easy to think that we all have enough of everything in our kitchens. How can we possibly fit one more appliance onto our crowded kitchen counter top? Well, after creating and testing hundreds of recipes for the *Ninja™ Blender*, we want to share our little secret with you right now...sweep all other appliances and prep tools aside and place your *Ninja™ Blender* squarely up front and in the center of your counter because you'll use it every single day.

What makes this blender, and the accessories that come with it, so essential in your kitchen? The first thing we noticed while prepping recipes is that it actually performs like a champ. Your ice cubes will turn into crystal-smooth shaved powder, your soups will be creamy and smooth, smoothies are uniformly frosty, and all of your salsas and veggie mixes will be uniformly chopped to perfection. And, one of the best features of all is that the blade assembly is removable so that you can actually use your spatula to get into every corner of the pitcher or bowl when you're done blending.

In this cookbook you'll find a wide variety of recipes for every day — entrées, appetizers, smoothies, cocktails, desserts and more. We know that once you get started with some of these recipes, you'll simply toss your own imaginative creations into the blender and produce custom smoothies, shakes and cocktails all your own. You'll find creative ways to speed through your favorite recipes using the fast prep *Ninja™ Blender* and you'll discover some new recipes to delight your entire household. We hope you enjoy your *Ninja™ Blender* and these recipes as much as we do. We've had so much fun working with this blender and we know you will, too. Get ready for some delicious and delightful blending experiences!

Deb Rousson
Connie Neckels

SECRETS TO SUCCESS WITH YOUR NINJA™ BLENDER

DURING THE PROCESS of creating these recipes, we've discovered some short-cuts and secrets to recipe success. We like to share them with you:

• The results of your recipe will depend on how well you measure the ingredients. Using dry and fluid measuring cups when needed and measuring with measuring spoons (instead of that random spoon out of your drawer) will guarantee a success.

• One of the best features of the *Ninja™ Blender* is the blade assembly that can be removed before pouring or spooning out ingredients. We love this feature! Be sure to handle the assembly very carefully, however, because it is extremely sharp. Children should not handle the blade assembly for any reason.

• When a recipe calls for more than 1 cup of flour, add the first cup and blend briefly. Continue adding flour 1 cup at a time to ensure that the dough or batter evenly absorbs the flour. Stop the blender and clean the sides of the pitcher or bowl as needed. Invest in a good quality, flexible plastic spatula for easy clean-ups.

• Use speed ❶ whenever you are using the dough blade or the dough paddle. Speed ❶ is perfect for the gradual incorporation of ingredients in batters and doughs. Do not use speed ❷ or ❸ while using the dough blade or dough paddle.

• It's a toss-up whether or not to strain fruit and vegetable juices before drinking them. Use a fine sieve for straining if beverages seem too thick, or strain half the juice and leave the rest intact and then blend together.

• As tempting as it may be to rush through your prep time, don't overfill your *Ninja™ Blender* with too much liquid; use the maximum fill line as your absolute guide.

• Avoid any splatters by loosely covering the pour tab with a small towel as you add ingredients while the blender is running.

SWEET
STRAWBERRY
SMOOTHIE
P. 22

CHAPTER ONE

Juice Blends
& Smoothies

BREAKFAST VEGGIE BLEND

SERVES 1

A powerful antioxidant breakfast blend!

1 cup vegetable blend juice
¼ cup fresh carrot, cut into chunks
8 leaves fresh spinach, torn
pinch salt
pinch black pepper

Place all of the ingredients into the bowl. Blend on ③ until smooth. Pour and serve over ice.

✳ TIP

For extra protein power, add up to ½ cup packed spinach leaves. You'll have energy for the whole day!

YOU'LL NEED:

✓ 40 ounce Bowl
✓ Blade Assembly
✓ Bowl Lid

GARDEN IN A GLASS

SERVES 1

Serve icy-cold as an appetizer or chilled as a refreshing beverage. The combined flavors of this blend are very soothing on a hot summer day.

8 ounces spicy tomato juice
1 teaspoon lemon juice
1 small Roma tomato, cut into quarters
1-inch piece onion, peeled
1-inch piece green bell pepper, seeded
dash Tabasco® sauce
celery stick for garnish

Pour the tomato and lemon juices into the bowl. Add the tomato, onion and green pepper. Add the Tabasco sauce to taste. Blend on ② for 1 minute, or until very smooth. Strain, if desired, and pour over ice into a tall glass. Garnish with the celery stick.

✳TIP

Although many people prefer strained juices, unstrained juices contain more fiber and are better for you – give it a try!

YOU'LL NEED:

✓ 40 ounce Bowl
✓ Blade Assembly
✓ Bowl Lid

FRESH TOMATO JUICE

SERVES 4

If you have a bag of just-picked tomatoes, or have just left the farmer's market, blend fresh tomatoes into this remarkably good-for-you juice. The only question is whether or not you'll choose to strain this juice, but either way, it's delicious.

1 pound large, ripe tomatoes, cored and seeded, cut into chunks
2 ribs celery, cut into large pieces
pinch sea salt
pinch black pepper
celery sticks

Place the tomatoes, celery, salt and pepper in a saucepan and simmer over medium heat for approximately 25 minutes, stirring occasionally. Break up large pieces with a spoon as the tomatoes heat. Remove from the heat and pour the mixture into the pitcher. Be careful to avoid splashing the hot liquid onto your hands or face.

Blend the tomato mixture on ❷ until smooth. If desired, strain the juice through a fine sieve to remove any remaining particles or omit this step if you prefer a more textured juice. Fill 4 juice glasses with ice and pour the juice over each. Garnish each with a celery stick.

YOU'LL NEED:

√ 72 ounce Pitcher
√ Blade Assembly
√ Pitcher Lid

SPARKLING LEMONADE WITH FRESH BASIL

SERVES 6 TO 8

Perfect for a kitchen full of thirsty kids!

3 fresh lemons, peeled, seeded and cut into chunks
6 ounce can frozen lemonade concentrate,
undiluted
28 ounces club soda
1 liter ginger ale
fresh basil sprigs for garnish

Place the lemons, lemonade concentrate and 2 cups of the club soda into the pitcher. Blend on ② until smooth. Strain the juice through a fine sieve. Pour the juice into a large pitcher and add the remaining club soda and ginger ale. Stir well to combine. Pour the juice over ice and garnish each serving with basil.

✳ TIP

Freeze fresh strawberries and float a few in each glass as a garnish.

YOU'LL NEED:

√ 72 ounce Pitcher
√ Blade Assembly
√ Pitcher Lid

APPLE, CARROT & GINGER TEA

SERVES 2

The tart-sweet combinations in this tea are smooth and refreshing. Fresh ginger can be overwhelming, so start with just a little and add more as you prefer.

1 small green apple, peeled, cored and chunked
1 carrot peeled and cut into chunks
2 cups prepared iced tea
1 teaspoon sugar
pinch fresh ginger, grated

Place the apple and carrot into a microwave-safe bowl and add ¼ cup water. Microwave on High for 3 to 5 minutes, or until the apple and carrot are soft. Place the apple, carrot and juice, along with all of the remaining ingredients into the pitcher. Blend on ③ until smooth. Remove and strain the tea through a fine sieve. Pour the tea over ice cubes into tall glasses and serve at once.

✳ TIP

Fresh ginger has been used for centuries in China, where it is prized for both its flavor and the soothing effect it has on the digestive system.

YOU'LL NEED:

✓ **72 ounce Pitcher**
✓ **Blade Assembly**
✓ **Pitcher Lid**

RULE THE KITCHEN

APPLE & PINEAPPLE JUICE BLEND

MAKES ABOUT 6 CUPS OF JUICE BLEND

Cooking the apples first allows the fruit flavor to mellow and sweeten naturally.

4 cooking apples, peeled and cored
½ cup fresh pineapple, cut in chunks
½ teaspoon ground cinnamon
4 cups apple juice

Place the apples and the pineapple in a microwave-safe bowl and add 2 tablespoons of water. Cover with plastic wrap and cook on High for 6 minutes, or until very tender. Spoon the mixture into the pitcher and add the cinnamon.

Blend the mixture on ②until smooth. Depending on your preference, pour the mixture through a fine sieve and add to the apple juice, or combine the apple/pineapple mixture with the juice and serve as is. Refrigerate any leftover juice.

✳TIP

If you like the fresh flavor of a homemade applesauce, change up this recipe by omitting the apple juice while blending. The results will be a sweet and sassy apple-pineapple sauce!

YOU'LL NEED:

✓ **72 ounce Pitcher**
✓ **Blade Assembly**
✓ **Pitcher Lid**

FRESH PEAR & MANGO NECTAR

SERVES 4 TO 6

Pears and mangos blend into an incredibly fresh-tasting and lightly sweet juice. Place your ripe pears in the refrigerator until use so that the juice will be clear instead of cloudy.

6 ripe pears, cored and cut into large pieces

4 cups mango nectar

Place the pears in a large microwave-safe bowl and add 2 tablespoons of water. Cook on High for 3 to 4 minutes, or until very tender. Remove and cool slightly.

Place half of the pears and nectar into the pitcher and blend on ❷ until uniformly smooth. Strain the juice through a fine sieve and pour into a large container or pitcher. Repeat with the remaining nectar and pears. Serve over ice or chill until ready to serve.

TIP

Look for mango nectar sold in cans in the juice or health food aisle of your grocery store.

YOU'LL NEED:

✓ **72 ounce Pitcher**
✓ **Blade Assembly**
✓ **Pitcher Lid**

PINEAPPLE BANANA SWIRL

SERVES 2

Start with pineapples and bananas; then add any other fruit you have on hand. Be ready to share this wonderfully fresh juice!

2 cups fresh pineapple, cut into pieces
1 banana, peeled, cut in half
2 cups pineapple juice

Place all ingredients in the pitcher. Blend on ③ for 20 seconds, or until smooth. Remove and serve or, if desired, strain through a fine sieve before serving.

✳TIP

Add strawberries, raspberries, boysenberries or blueberries for a seasonal treat!

YOU'LL NEED:

✓ **72 ounce Pitcher**
✓ **Blade Assembly**
✓ **Pitcher Lid**

ORANGE DOUBLE-UP

SERVES 4 TO 6

Packed with vitamin C, this juice will be as tart and as sweet as the oranges you choose.

4 cups orange juice, divided
½ cup frozen orange juice concentrate
2 medium fresh oranges, peeled, seeded and cut into pieces
16 ounces carbonated water

Pour 2 cups of orange juice into the pitcher. Add the juice concentrate and the fresh oranges. Blend on ② until uniformly smooth. Pour the mixture into a large serving pitcher and add the remaining orange juice and carbonated water. Stir well to blend. Pour over ice and serve.

TIP

This bubbly juice blend can serve as a special breakfast or brunch drink for kids in lieu of champagne punch or mimosas. Serve in plastic champagne flutes for even more flair!

YOU'LL NEED:

✓ **72 ounce Pitcher**
✓ **Blade Assembly**
✓ **Pitcher Lid**

VEGGIE IRON POWER PUNCH

SERVES 1

The sweetened tea and apple slices add a hint of sugar to this iron-packed spinach tea.

2 cups cold iced tea, sweetened
8 leaves spinach, washed
1 rib celery
½ green apple, cut into pieces

Pour the tea into the bowl and add the spinach, celery and green apple. Blend on ② until smooth. Strain the drink through a fine sieve and serve in a tall glass over ice.

✳ TIP

Start by adding 8 leaves to this recipe and, as you adapt to the flavor, increase the fresh spinach leaves up to ½ cup packed. Spinach equals energy!

YOU'LL NEED:

✓ 40 ounce Bowl
✓ Blade Assembly
✓ Bowl Lid

HOT APPLE CHERRY CIDER WITH CINNAMON CRÈME

SERVES 4 TO 6

Float an island of silky, light cinnamon-laced crème on top of warm cider!

1 pint heavy whipping cream
2 tablespoons sugar
pinch ground cinnamon
6 ounces maraschino cherries, drained, stems and pits removed
32 ounces prepared hot apple cider

Pour the whipping cream into the pitcher. Whip on ③ until soft peaks form, about 35 seconds. Remove the cream from the pitcher and fold in the sugar and cinnamon with a plastic spatula.

Clean the pitcher and dry. Place the cherries in the pitcher and blend on ① for 10 seconds, or until uniformly smooth. To serve, spoon equal portions of the cherries into heatproof glasses, pour the hot apple cider over the cherries and top each with a large dollop of the cinnamon crème. Serve right away.

YOU'LL NEED:

✓ **72 ounce Pitcher**
✓ **Blade Assembly**
✓ **Pitcher Lid**

RULE THE KITCHEN

MANGO, PAPAYA & BANANA NECTAR

SERVES 2 TO 3

This gentle reminder of the tropics is a delicious break from typical juice blends.

½ cup ripe mango, cut into chunks
½ cup ripe papaya, cut into slices
½ ripe banana, cut into chunks
16 ounces guava nectar

Place the fruit in the pitcher and add the nectar. Blend on ② until smooth. Pour into small glasses and serve right away.

✳ TIP

Double this recipe easily for a crowd-pleasing juice blend!

YOU'LL NEED:

✓ 72 ounce Pitcher
✓ Blade Assembly
✓ Pitcher Lid

RAISIN-TOPPED CARROT SMOOTHIE

SERVES 2

You'll be reminded of carrot cake with cream cheese frosting!

2 large fresh carrots, peeled and cut into chunks
2 tablespoons water
3 cups apple juice
6 ounces lowfat vanilla-flavored yogurt
2 ounces cream cheese
1 cup ice cubes
2 tablespoons golden raisins for garnish

Place the carrots in a glass or plastic bowl and add the water. Cover with a paper towel and microwave on high power for 3 minutes, or until the carrots are tender when pierced with a fork. Remove, drain the water and discard, and set the carrots aside to cool slightly.

Place the carrots in the pitcher and add the apple juice. Blend on ❶ for 20 seconds (to cool the carrots completely). Add the yogurt, cream cheese and ice cubes and blend on ❸ until the mixture is very smooth. If needed, clean the sides of the pitcher with a spatula and blend again. Pour the smoothie into large glasses and top with the golden raisins as a garnish. Serve right away.

YOU'LL NEED:

✓ **72 ounce Pitcher**
✓ **Blade Assembly**
✓ **Pitcher Lid**

RULE THE KITCHE

SWEET STRAWBERRY SMOOTHIE

SERVES 2 TO 3

This recipe invites you to add a little bit of cream to your strawberries, so why not add some rich decadence to your day?

½ cup half-and-half cream
½ cup whole milk
1 cup ripe, sweet strawberries, stemmed and washed
½ cup lowfat vanilla-flavored yogurt
2 cups ice cubes

Pour the cream and milk into the pitcher and add the strawberries, yogurt and ice cubes. Blend on ③ until the mixture is very smooth and no fruit pieces remain. Pour into glasses and serve right away.

✳ TIP

This smoothie is the perfect "starter" recipe and probably the most favorite of all for most smoothie lovers. Change it to suit yourself by adding your favorite fruit or other sweet flavors, a little bit at a time.

YOU'LL NEED:

✓ 72 ounce Pitcher
✓ Blade Assembly
✓ Pitcher Lid

BANANA PINEAPPLE SMOOTHIE

SERVES 3 TO 4

Just a hint of coconut plays against the tart pineapple and smooth banana flavors.

2 cups pineapple juice
1 cup pineapple chunks, fresh or canned
1 small ripe banana, cut into chunks
¼ cup unsweetened coconut milk
1 tablespoon honey
3 cups ice cubes

Pour the juice into the pitcher and add the pineapple, banana, coconut milk, honey and ice. Blend on ③ until very smooth. Pour into glasses and serve at once.

✳ TIP

If you can't find unsweetened coconut milk, substitute sweetened milk and omit the honey.

YOU'LL NEED:

✓ **72 ounce Pitcher**
✓ **Blade Assembly**
✓ **Pitcher Lid**

RULE THE KITCHEN

TRIPLE BERRY TWIST

SERVES 3 TO 4

Substitute any fresh, ripe berries…and create a new twist of your own.

½ cup fresh, ripe raspberries
½ cup fresh, ripe blackberries
½ cup fresh, ripe strawberries
½ cup fat-free, non-dairy vanilla coffee creamer
½ cup lowfat or nonfat milk
1 tablespoon sugar or sugar substitute
3 cups ice cubes

Place the fruit in the pitcher and add the creamer, milk and sugar. Add the ice cubes and blend on ③ until completely smooth. Serve right away.

TIP

This recipe is perfect if you are watching your fat and calorie counts!

YOU'LL NEED:

√ 72 ounce Pitcher
√ Blade Assembly
√ Pitcher Lid

SUMMER SWEET PEACH SMOOTHIE

SERVES 2 TO 3

There's really no substitute for fresh peaches in this smoothie so make this when the peach trees are hanging heavy with their luscious fruit. Use very ripe, soft peaches and add a bit of ground ginger if you're feeling adventurous.

2 ripe, sweet peaches, pitted and peeled
1 cup lowfat peach-flavored yogurt
1 cup peach nectar, chilled
2½ cups ice cubes

Place all ingredients into the pitcher. Blend on ❸ until completely smooth. Pour into glasses and serve right away.

✳ TIP

Chill a travel mug in your freezer and pour your smoothie into the mug before your commute to work in the morning. The mug will keep your smoothie frosty cold for many miles!

YOU'LL NEED:

✓ 72 ounce Pitcher
✓ Blade Assembly
✓ Pitcher Lid

RULE THE KITCHEN

HOT CRANBERRY SOOTHER

SERVES 4

A tasty relief when coffee and tea become tiresome.

½ cup canned cranberry jelly
4 cups cranberry juice cocktail
1 ripe orange, peeled and seeded, cut into chunks
pinch ground cinnamon
pinch ground cloves

Spoon the cranberry jelly into the pitcher and add the juice and orange pieces. Blend on ③ until smooth. If desired, strain the mixture through a fine sieve.

Pour the mixture into a saucepan and add the cinnamon and cloves. Heat until warmed through. Ladle into mugs and serve.

TIP

We think of this tart and sweet hot drink as soon as the nights start to turn crisp and cold and frost is on the roof in the morning.

YOU'LL NEED:

✓ **72 ounce Pitcher**
✓ **Blade Assembly**
✓ **Pitcher Lid**

TANGERINE TANGO

SERVES 4 TO 6

Add a shot of dark rum as a sure remedy against a freezing winter's evening.

3 ripe tangerines or mandarin oranges,
peeled and seeded
1 ripe tangerine (or mandarin),
peeled and thinly sliced
8 cups apple juice, divided
1 tablespoon dark brown sugar

Place the 3 tangerines in the pitcher and add 2 cups of the apple juice. Blend on ③ until the fruit is uniform. Strain the juice through a fine sieve.

In a medium saucepan, heat the blended tangerine and apple juice, remaining apple juice and sugar until steaming. Stir occasionally. Place one slice of tangerine in the bottom of individual mugs and ladle the hot juice over the slices. Serve while hot.

✳ TIP

Use very ripe tangerines or mandarin oranges for the best burst of flavor in this special drink.

YOU'LL NEED:

√ **72 ounce Pitcher**
√ **Blade Assembly**
√ **Pitcher Lid**

HOT CHAI TEA

SERVES 2

This is a mix of the traditional and the new chai tea methods of preparation. Don't skimp on the spices; when crushed, they add a tremendous boost of flavor.

2 cups half and half cream
¼ inch piece fresh ginger, peeled
¼ teaspoon ground cinnamon
1 pod cardamom
1 teaspoon sugar
2 cups water
2 tablespoons black tea, loose or in bag

Place the cream, ginger, cinnamon and cardamom in the pitcher. Blend on **1** for 20 seconds. Add the sugar and water and blend again for 10 seconds. Pour the tea into a medium saucepan and heat until the liquid begins to bubble around the edges. Continue heating on a low simmer for 2 minutes, stirring occasionally. Remove from the heat and immediately add the black tea and let stand for 1 minute. Strain through a fine sieve and serve right away.

✳TIP

Don't bother paying high coffeehouse prices for this delicate tea. It only takes a few minutes to prepare in your *Ninja™ blender* and the process of simmering the tea over low heat is calming in itself.

YOU'LL NEED:

✓ **72 ounce Pitcher**
✓ **Blade Assembly**
✓ **Pitcher Lid**

ORANGE RUSSIAN TEA

SERVES 1

Try this soothing tea whenever you have a sore throat or cold – it's practically medicinal.

1 cup water
1 teaspoon instant unsweetened iced tea
1 cup orange juice
1 teaspoon whole cloves
½ inch piece whole cinnamon
1 pod cardamom

Place all ingredients into the bowl. Blend on ❸ for 20 seconds. Strain the tea through a fine sieve. Microwave or heat in a saucepan on the stove until steaming.

✳TIP

Make this for a crowd by adjusting the ingredient amounts and add a shot of honey-based Canadian whiskey (such as Yukon Jack™) per serving for a kick of warmth!

YOU'LL NEED:

✓ **40 ounce Bowl**
✓ **Blade Assembly**
✓ **Bowl Lid**

FROSTY
ORANGE CREAM
P. 36

CHAPTER TWO
Frozen Drink
Specialties

MOCHA FREEZE

SERVES 4

Keeping instant cocoa and coffee in your pantry ensures that you'll always have the ingredients for this delicious frozen drink at hand.

⅓ cup instant cocoa mix
2 tablespoons instant coffee
¼ cup sugar
¼ cup hot water
1 quart lowfat milk, partially frozen until chunky

In a small bowl, mix together the cocoa mix, coffee and sugar. Add the hot water and stir to blend well.

Pour the mixture into the pitcher. Add the partially frozen milk to the pitcher. Blend on ❸ until very smooth. Pour into 4 glasses and serve at once.

✳ TIP

The partially frozen milk used in this recipe takes the place of ice cubes. You can easily add protein and calcium to your diet by interchanging frozen milk for any recipes that call for ice cubes. You'll get the same smooth and icy results.

YOU'LL NEED:

✓ 72 ounce Pitcher
✓ Blade Assembly
✓ Pitcher Lid

BLAST O' BERRIES SHAKE

SERVES 3 TO 4

Caramelized strawberries provide the naturally sweet and fruity flavor for this shake.

1 tablespoon butter
2 cups strawberries, cleaned and hulled, sliced
¼ cup lowfat milk
1 teaspoon pure vanilla extract
4 cups premium vanilla ice cream

Place the butter in a saucepan and add the strawberries. Heat over medium-low, stirring occasionally, for 5 minutes, to caramelize the fruit. Do not allow the fruit to brown or burn. Remove from the heat and let cool.

Place the cooled strawberries, milk and vanilla in the pitcher. Blend on **1** until smooth. Add the ice cream and blend on **3** until smooth. Spoon into glasses and serve right away.

✳TIP

Try this with caramelized blackberries, boysenberries or raspberries as well.

YOU'LL NEED:

✓ **72 ounce Pitcher**
✓ **Blade Assembly**
✓ **Pitcher Lid**

RULE THE KITCHE

MOCHA AT MIDNIGHT SHAKE

SERVES 2 (LARGE) OR 4 (SMALL)

The perfect answer to a midnight raid on the freezer.

¼ cup half and half cream
¼ cup cold prepared coffee
¼ cup prepared hot fudge topping
3½ cups premium chocolate ice cream

Pour the cream and coffee into the pitcher. Blend on **1** for a few seconds. Add the fudge topping and the ice cream. Blend on **3** until smooth and frosty. Pour or spoon into glasses and serve right away.

❋ TIP

It's easy to create a "lighter" version of this decadent shake – use lowfat milk, chocolate syrup and chocolate frozen yogurt to cut the calories and fat in half.

YOU'LL NEED:

✓ 72 ounce Pitcher
✓ Blade Assembly
✓ Pitcher Lid

CARAMEL CRÈME PARFAITS

SERVES 4

Delicate cream and silky, rich caramel –
the perfect pairing.

1 cup heavy whipping cream
1 teaspoon sugar
4 cups premium vanilla ice cream
½ cup premium caramel sauce, divided
½ cup lowfat milk

Pour the cream into the pitcher and whip on **3** until stiff peaks form, about 35 seconds. Gently fold in the sugar and set aside. Clean the pitcher and dry.

Place the ice cream and ¼ cup of caramel sauce into the pitcher. Add the milk and blend on **3** until very smooth. Remove and assemble the parfaits. Drizzle a small amount of the remaining caramel sauce down the sides of 4 glasses. Layer the ice cream and whipped cream into each glass. Top each parfait with a drizzle of the remaining caramel sauce and serve at once.

✳TIP

For an interesting twist, add a layer or two of fresh sliced strawberries or crumbled granola to these deliciously rich parfaits.

YOU'LL NEED:

✓ **72 ounce Pitcher**
✓ **Blade Assembly**
✓ **Pitcher Lid**

FROSTY ORANGE CREAM

SERVES 2 TO 3

Cold, tart and creamy!

12 ounces lowfat milk, chilled
¼ cup frozen orange juice concentrate
1 teaspoon vanilla extract
2 tablespoons sugar
3 cups ice cubes

Pour the milk into the pitcher and add the orange juice concentrate, vanilla and sugar. Blend on ❶ for a few seconds. Add the ice cubes and blend on ❸ until frosty and smooth. Pour into glasses and serve right away.

✳TIP

This recipe is a variation of a well-known orange cream drink and it captures that same delicious fruit and cream flavor tango. We did not add egg to froth this as is commonly included, but you can always add one egg for extra energy and protein.

YOU'LL NEED:

✓ 72 ounce Pitcher
✓ Blade Assembly
✓ Pitcher Lid

SOY LATTE FREEZE

SERVES 3 TO 4

A nice change of pace from the typical coffeehouse drink.

¾ cup vanilla-flavored soymilk (regular or light)
2 shots espresso coffee, at room temperature
1 tablespoon sugar
3 cups ice cubes

Pour the soymilk and coffee into the pitcher. Add the sugar and blend for a few seconds. Add the ice cubes and blend on ❸ until very smooth. Pour into glasses and serve right away.

✳TIP

Change it up to almond milk or nonfat dairy creamer in place of the soymilk. Each little change results in refreshing, new flavors.

YOU'LL NEED:

✓ 72 ounce Pitcher
✓ Blade Assembly
✓ Pitcher Lid

RULE THE KITCH

DUO DARK CHOCOLATE FRAPPE

SERVES 4

Decadently rich, but decidedly easy.

½ cup dark chocolate fudge sauce
½ cup chocolate milk
1 cup ice cubes
3 cups premium fudge ice cream

Prepare 4 tall glasses by pouring the fudge sauce in ribbons down the sides of each glass. Set aside.

Pour the milk into the pitcher and add the ice cubes. Blend on ❸ until smooth. Add the fudge ice cream and blend again on ❸. Use a spatula to clean the sides of the pitcher, if needed, and blend again on ❸ until completely smooth.

Pour the frappe into each prepared glass and serve at once.

TIP

Half the fun of this recipe is seeing the rich chocolate ribbons running down the sides of the glasses. Use the fanciest glassware you have or try champagne flutes or even stemmed wineglasses.

YOU'LL NEED:

✓ 72 ounce Pitcher
✓ Blade Assembly
✓ Pitcher Lid

ICED TROPICAL RAINBOW

MAKES 4 SMALL SERVINGS

Your *Ninja™ Blender* will perfectly turn ice cubes into snowy-white ice powder. Top off with flavors of your choice for a tropical blast!

4 cups ice cubes
3 flavored syrups (such as Torani®)
(we suggest: blue raspberry, pineapple, and mango)

Place the ice cubes in the pitcher and blend on ❸ until a very uniform powder is formed. Using a large spoon, lightly pack the ice powder into 4 small cups or glasses. Pour 1 ounce each of three different flavored syrups over the top of each serving. Serve at once.

☀TIP

Keep several flavored syrups on hand in your pantry for the hottest summer days when your kids will appreciate this icy treat. If you want to really impress your kids, serve in classic white paper cone cups, available at kitchen supply stores.

YOU'LL NEED:

✓ 72 ounce Pitcher
✓ Blade Assembly
✓ Pitcher Lid

PINEAPPLE & MANGO FROSTEE

SERVES 2 TO 3

This frozen drink has an added boost of nutritional value with fresh fruit and calcium. Enjoy!

1 cup fresh pineapple, cut in large pieces
1 cup mango, cut into large pieces
½ cup lowfat milk
1 teaspoon honey
1 pint mango sorbet

Place the pineapple and mango in the pitcher and add the milk. Blend on **2** for about 10 seconds, or until smooth. Add the honey and sorbet and blend on **3** until smooth. Pour into 2 glasses and serve at once.

TIP

Use any kind of sorbet you have on hand – pineapple, orange, raspberry – everything works in this luscious recipe!

YOU'LL NEED:

✓ 72 ounce Pitcher
✓ Blade Assembly
✓ Pitcher Lid

RULE THE KITCHEN

CHOCOLATE MINT CHIP MILKSHAKE

SERVES 3

Thick and rich – a classic milkshake in a minute.

½ cup semi-sweet chocolate chip pieces
4 cups mint ice cream
½ cup lowfat milk
mint leaves for garnish

Place the chocolate chip pieces in the pitcher and blend on **1** for a few seconds until the chips are uniformly chopped. Add the ice cream and milk and blend on **3** until smooth.

Pour or spoon the milkshake into tall glasses and garnish each glass with mint leaves before serving.

✳TIP

Toss white or milk chocolate chips in just about any dessert drink for a sweet change.

YOU'LL NEED:

√ 72 ounce Pitcher
√ Blade Assembly
√ Pitcher Lid

BLACK CHERRY FREEZE

SERVES 3 TO 4

Dark, sweet cherries combine with sparkling soda to make this special frozen drink.

1 pint ripe dark cherries, pitted and cut in half
6 cups lemon-lime soda, divided
2 cups ice cubes

Place the cherries and ½ cup of soda in the pitcher. Blend on **2** for 1 minute until smooth. Add the remainder of the soda and the ice cubes. Blend on **3** until very smooth. Serve in tall glasses.

✳ TIP

Switch the lemon-lime soda to cola for a cherry cola blast to the past.

YOU'LL NEED:

✓ 72 ounce Pitcher
✓ Blade Assembly
✓ Pitcher Lid

FROZEN CHOCOLATE CHEESECAKE

SERVES 4

Classic chocolate cheesecake – in an ice-cold drink.

1 cup heavy cream
1 teaspoon sugar
¼ cup whole milk
½ cup cream cheese (whipped or regular)
3½ cups premium chocolate ice cream
¼ cup raspberry jam

Pour the heavy cream into the pitcher and whip on ❸ until peaks form, about 35 seconds. Remove the cream from the pitcher and fold in the sugar. Place in the refrigerator until use. Clean and dry the pitcher.

Pour the milk into the pitcher and add the cream cheese. Pulse for a few seconds to blend. Add the chocolate ice cream and blend on ❸ until very smooth. Spoon the mixture into 4 small glasses.

Top each serving with a dollop of raspberry jam and the whipped cream. Serve at once.

✳TIP

Substitute lowfat cream cheese, lowfat chocolate frozen yogurt, lowfat milk and light cream if you want to cut about fifty percent of the calories and fat – without losing the luscious flavor – in this easy recipe.

YOU'LL NEED:

✓ 72 ounce Pitcher
✓ Blade Assembly
✓ Pitcher Lid

BLACK & TAN SWIRL

SERVES 4

If vanilla ice cream with chocolate syrup is called a "Black & White," then this creamy combination of vanilla ice cream, chocolate syrup and caramel must be a "Black & Tan."

½ cup half and half cream
3 cups premium vanilla ice cream
1 cup premium fudge ice cream
½ cup caramel syrup
½ cup thin chocolate syrup (such as Hersey's™)

Pour the cream into the pitcher and add the vanilla and fudge ice cream. Blend on ❸ until very smooth. Swirl a few tablespoons of caramel syrup into each of 4 glasses. Swirl 2 tablespoons of the chocolate syrup over the top of the caramel. Spoon the chocolate milkshake into each glass over the syrups and serve at once.

TIP

Substitute coffee ice cream in place of the fudge ice cream. Try topping with coffee beans, chopped pecans or hazelnuts!

YOU'LL NEED:

✓ 72 ounce Pitcher
✓ Blade Assembly
✓ Pitcher Lid

RULE THE KITCHEN

CANDY BAR CRUNCH

SERVES 4

Seems like a match made in heaven – crunchy chocolate candy and sweet vanilla ice cream!

3 large chocolate candy bars with almonds or peanuts
3½ cups premium vanilla or chocolate ice cream
½ cup milk
slivered almonds or chopped peanuts for garnish

Place the candy bars in the pitcher and add the ice cream and milk. Blend on ❸ until the candy is uniformly chopped and the drink is smooth. Spoon into glasses and garnish each serving with nuts, if preferred.

✳ TIP

The list of candy bars to use in this recipe is endless. Try any chocolate/nut combinations or look for nougat/nut bars and toffee/nut specialties. The *Ninja™ blender* will smoothly blend your favorite flavors.

YOU'LL NEED:

✓ 72 ounce Pitcher
✓ Blade Assembly
✓ Pitcher Lid

ROCKY ROAD SHAKE

SERVES 4

Make any number of substitutions in this recipe to create your own favorite. Try swapping the nuts or ice cream flavors, or add candied or dried fruit.

½ cup lowfat milk
4 cups premium chocolate ice cream
1 cup miniature marshmallows
¼ cup maraschino cherries, pitted, stems removed
¼ cup walnuts, halved

Pour the milk into the pitcher and add the ice cream. Add the marshmallows, cherries and walnuts. Blend on ❸ for about 20 seconds, or until the ingredients are uniformly chopped and the drink is fairly smooth.

Spoon into glasses and serve at once.

✳TIP

Rocky road ice cream used to be a staple at the corner drug store and, although tastes have become more sophisticated these days, there is still something very satisfying about the taste of nuts mixed with sweet cherries and marshmallows wrapped up in melty ice cream.

YOU'LL NEED:

✓ 72 ounce Pitcher
✓ Blade Assembly
✓ Pitcher Lid

RULE THE KITCHE

PURE VANILLA MALT

SERVES 2

Simply perfection – without any other ingredients!

½ cup lowfat milk
3 cups premium vanilla ice cream
¼ cup malted milk powder
½ teaspoon vanilla extract

Pour the milk into the pitcher and add the ice cream, malted milk powder and vanilla extract. Blend on ❸ until smooth and creamy. Pour into 2 large glasses and serve at once.

✳TIP

Use this simple recipe as the starting place for all your favorite additions – think fresh fruit, nuts, dark chocolate, butterscotch, specialty candies, sandwich cookies, and more. Toss in chocolate malt balls, too!

YOU'LL NEED:

✓ 72 ounce Pitcher
✓ Blade Assembly
✓ Pitcher Lid

ESPRESSO ICE CREAM FREEZE

SERVES 3 TO 4

This frozen drink salutes coffee in three perfect ways – espresso coffee, coffee beans, and coffee ice cream.

2 shots espresso coffee, at room temperature
¼ cup chocolate-covered espresso beans
¼ cup milk
4 cups premium coffee ice cream

Pour the coffee into the pitcher and add the espresso beans. Blend on **2** until the beans are uniformly chopped. Add the milk and ice cream and blend on 3 until thick and smooth. Spoon into tall glass mugs and serve right away.

YOU'LL NEED:

✓ **72 ounce Pitcher**
✓ **Blade Assembly**
✓ **Pitcher Lid**

RULE THE KITCHEN

FROZEN
BLUE BAYOU
P. 52

CHAPTER THREE

Cocktails & Party Drinks

FROZEN BLUE BAYOU

MAKES 4 TO 6 SERVINGS

This cool refresher is made with Blue Curacao, an orange flavored liqueur that originated in the Caribbean. It is now produced mainly in France and is available in many colors.

4 cups ice cubes, crushed
6 ounces good quality vodka
4 ounces Blue Curacao
2 cups lemonade
4 to 6 frozen lime wedges for garnish

Place the ice into the pitcher and add the remaining ingredients, except the lime wedges. Blend on **3** until smooth. Pour into tall chilled glasses and garnish with lime wedges.

✳ TIP

Invest in a bottle of Blue Curacao, which is reasonably priced, for a splash of color and flavor at your next party. The vivid blue color alone invites a happy response from each guest!

YOU'LL NEED:

✓ 72 ounce Pitcher
✓ Blade Assembly
✓ Pitcher Lid

THE KITCHEN

THE PERFECT BLENDED MARGARITA

MAKES 4 SERVINGS

It's hard to make a mistake when using a can to measure the ingredients; clever and very, very good!

12 ounce can frozen limeade
1 can good quality tequila
⅓ can triple sec
½ can fresh lime juice
½ can water
4 cups crushed ice cubes

Garnish
½ cup coarse salt for garnish
4 lime slices for garnish

Place all ingredients into pitcher and blend on ❸ until smooth. Pour the salt onto a shallow saucer. Moisten the rim of each margarita glass with lime juice, then dip the rim of the glass in the salt. Fill prepared glasses with the blended margarita and garnish with a slice of lime.

✳ TIP

Don't skimp on the special touches, such as coarse salt and slices of lime. The little garnishes make all the difference in this popular drink.

YOU'LL NEED:

✓ 72 ounce Pitcher
✓ Blade Assembly
✓ Pitcher Lid

RULE THE KITC

THE PERFECT TOP-SHELF MARGARITA ON THE ROCKS

MAKES 4 SERVINGS

The higher the quality of the alcohol, the higher shelf it occupies in many fine bars. This recipe calls for top quality alcohol, hence the name, Top-Shelf Margarita.

12 ounces good quality silver tequila
4 ounces orange flavored liqueur (Cointreau or Grand Marnier)
8 ounces fresh lime juice
4 cups crushed ice cubes

Garnish
½ cup coarse salt for garnish
4 lime slices

Pour tequila, Cointreau and fresh lime juice into the pitcher and pulse on ❶ until well-blended. Sprinkle the salt onto a shallow saucer. Moisten the rim of each margarita glass with the lime juice, then dip the rim of the glass in the salt. Add crushed ice cubes to prepared glasses and fill with the margarita. Garnish with a slice of lime.

TIP

Whether you are an "On the Rocks" purist or you love a smooth, frosty blended margarita, adding a float of Cointreau or Grand Marnier on top creates a lasting impression. Your guests will definitely be back for more.

YOU'LL NEED:

✓ 72 ounce Pitcher
✓ Blade Assembly
✓ Pitcher Lid

FRESH COCONUT PINA COLADA

MAKES 2 SERVINGS

The ultimate tropical vacation cocktail. Why not have a few friends over for a get-a-way in your own backyard?

2 cups crushed ice cubes
4 ounces light rum
2 ounces dark rum
¾ cup pineapple juice
4 ounces coconut milk
shaved fresh coconut for garnish

Place the ice into the pitcher and add the remaining ingredients, except the garnish. Blend on ❸ until smooth.

Pour into chilled glasses and garnish with the shaved fresh coconut. Serve with a straw.

✳ TIP

If you want to impress, serve with fresh pineapple spears dipped in milk chocolate. Wow!

YOU'LL NEED:

✓ 72 ounce Pitcher
✓ Blade Assembly
✓ Pitcher Lid

RULE THE KITC

FROZEN WHITE SANGRIA

MAKES 6 SERVINGS

To make this cool Spanish cocktail, you need to start the day before, as the fresh pineapple and oranges must be frozen.

1 cup crushed ice cubes
2 cups fresh pineapple, chopped, frozen
2 large oranges peeled and sectioned, frozen
2 cups dry white wine, chilled
½ cup brandy
½ cup orange flavored liqueur (triple sec or Grand Marnier)
6 mint sprigs for garnish

Place the chopped pineapple and orange on a baking sheet and freeze until firm, at least 12 hours.

Place the frozen fruit and the remaining ingredients, except the garnish, into the pitcher and blend on ❸ until smooth. Pour into individual glasses and garnish each with mint.

❋ TIP

Perfect for your next girls-night-out party! The frozen fruit really comes alive when blended with white wine, but the flavors are smooth. Double the recipe and use frozen fruit to float as garnishes.

THE KITCHEN®

YOU'LL NEED:

✓ 72 ounce Pitcher
✓ Blade Assembly
✓ Pitcher Lid

STRAWBERRY DAIQUIRI

MAKES 6 SERVINGS

As versatile as it is good, it's easy to substitute peaches, bananas, or your favorite fruit in this inviting drink.

8 ounces light rum
4 ounces fresh lime juice
2 tablespoons superfine sugar
2 cups hulled fresh strawberries
4 ounces orange flavored liqueur (triple sec, Cointreau or Grand Marnier)
4 cups crushed ice cubes

Garnish
6 whole strawberries, halved
2 kiwi, peeled and cut into 12 pieces
6 mint sprigs
6 thin wooden skewers

Place the rum, juice, sugar, strawberries and triple sec in the pitcher and blend on ❷ until smooth. Add the ice cubes and blend again on ❸ until very smooth.

Thread the strawberries and kiwi alternately onto skewers. Divide the daiquiris into 6 chilled glasses and garnish with fruit skewers and mint.

TIP

When entertaining kids, omit the rum and orange-flavored liqueur and substitute 8 ounces of lemon-lime soda and 1 tablespoon of rum flavoring instead. Garnish with the fruit skewers for an added splash.

YOU'LL NEED:

✓ 72 ounce Pitcher
✓ Blade Assembly
✓ Pitcher Lid

SEA BREEZE SOOTHER

MAKES 4 SERVINGS

To create a Hawaiian Sea Breeze, replace the grapefruit juice with pineapple juice.

1 cup good quality vodka
1½ cups cranberry juice
1½ cups grapefruit juice
4 cups crushed ice cubes
4 lime slices for garnish

Pour the vodka, cranberry juice and grapefruit juice into the pitcher and pulse on **1** until mixed and frothy.

Place the ice in chilled glasses, fill each with the drink and garnish with the lime slices.

✳ TIP

This is the perfect cocktail for those who prefer tart and tangy over sweet. Serve with southwestern foods or whole grain crackers and a cheese spread. The full flavor of this drink can accompany hearty foods without becoming overwhelmed.

YOU'LL NEED:

✓ 72 ounce Pitcher
✓ Blade Assembly
✓ Pitcher Lid

RULE THE KITC

PINEAPPLE MANGO MOJITO

MAKES 4 SERVINGS

It's hard to make a classic Mojito more tropical than it already is, but this really does the trick.

1 cup fresh pineapple chunks
1 cup fresh mango chunks
¼ cup fresh lime juice
2 tablespoons super-fine sugar
10 to 12 mint leaves
6 ounces light rum
2 cups sparkling water
4 cups ice cubes

Garnish
¼ cup superfine sugar
4 lime slices
4 sprigs of mint

Place the pineapple, mango, lime juice, sugar and mint into the pitcher and blend on **2** until smooth. Add the rum and 2 cups sparkling water and pulse until just blended.

Sprinkle the sugar onto a shallow saucer. Moisten the rim of each glass with lime and dip the rim of the glass into the sugar. Add the ice to the prepared glasses and fill each with the Pineapple Mango Mojito. Garnish with lime slices and a sprig of mint.

YOU'LL NEED:

✓ 72 ounce Pitcher
✓ Blade Assembly
✓ Pitcher Lid

LEMON MERINGUE

MAKES 2 SERVINGS

A fun twist on a Limoncello Martini.

3 ounces good quality citrus vodka
2 ounces Limoncello
1 ounce light Crème de Cacao

Place all ingredients into the pitcher and pulse on **1** to blend. Pour into chilled martini glasses and serve.

✳ TIP

Double or triple this recipe easily for a crowd and add mint for a garnish. This cocktail is especially good when the heat of the day hits the triple digits and then starts to cool in the evening.

YOU'LL NEED:

✓ 72 ounce Pitcher
✓ Blade Assembly
✓ Pitcher Lid

RULE THE KITC

FROZEN CUBAN MOJITO

MAKES 2 SERVINGS

This minty refresher will have you dreaming of Old Havana.

¼ cup simple syrup (recipe follows)
¼ cup fresh lime juice
10 fresh mint leaves
6 ounces light rum
3 cups crushed ice cubes
2 mint sprigs for garnish

Simple Syrup
½ cup water
½ cup sugar

Place the simple syrup, lime juice and mint leaves into the pitcher and pulse on ❶ until combined. Add the rum and crushed ice and blend on ❸ until smooth. Pour into rocks glasses and garnish with mint sprigs.

Simple Syrup: Combine water and sugar in a small sauce pan and bring to a boil. Simmer, while stirring, over low heat until the sugar dissolves. Cool to room temperature. Store in the refrigerator in a glass bottle.

YOU'LL NEED:

✓ 72 ounce Pitcher
✓ Blade Assembly
✓ Pitcher Lid

MILK CHOCOLATE MUDSLIDE

MAKES 4 SERVINGS

Can you say "Dessert?" These chocolate milkshakes are the ultimate treat!

4 ounces Kahlua
4 ounces Frangelico
4 ounces good quality vodka
4 large scoops chocolate ice cream
2 cups crushed ice cubes

Garnish
¼ cup superfine sugar
2 tablespoons powdered cocoa
4 chocolate rolled wafers

Place all ingredients, except the garnishes, into the pitcher and blend on ❸ until smooth.

In a small bowl, blend the superfine sugar and cocoa in a shallow saucer. Moisten the rim of each glass with Kahlua and dip the rim into the sugar cocoa mixture. Fill each glass with the drink and garnish with a rolled wafer.

✳ TIP

Substitute thin mint candy sticks as a garnish in this easy frozen cocktail.

YOU'LL NEED:

✓ 72 ounce Pitcher
✓ Blade Assembly
✓ Pitcher Lid

RULE THE KITC

ITALIAN BELLINI

MAKES 4 SERVINGS

The Bellini was invented in 1948 at Harry's Bar in Venice, Italy, a known hang-out of writer Ernest Hemingway.

6 medium white peaches, pitted and peeled
1 bottle Italian sparkling wine, chilled
(recommend Prosecco)
4 splashes Crème de framboise

Place the peaches into the pitcher and process on ❸ until uniformly smooth. Spoon the pureed peaches into four champagne flutes. Top the peach puree with a splash of Crème de framboise and fill with the Italian sparkling wine.

✳ TIP

For a touch of delight, serve these Bellinis with rich shortbread cookies.

YOU'LL NEED:

- ✓ 72 ounce Pitcher
- ✓ Blade Assembly
- ✓ Pitcher Lid

THE KITCHEN®

FROZEN LEMON DROP

SERVES 4

A twist on the popular martini named after a famous hard sugar candy.

4 cups crushed ice cubes
1 cup good quality vodka
1 cup lemon simple syrup (recipe follows)

Garnish
Superfine sugar
4 slices lemon
2 wedges of lemon

Lemon Simple Syrup
1 cup water
1 cup sugar
1½ cups fresh lemon juice

Place the ice into the pitcher, add the vodka and lemon simple syrup and blend on ❸ until smooth.

Sprinkle the sugar onto a shallow saucer. Moisten the rim of each martini glass with a lemon wedge, then dip the glass rim into the sugar. Pour the blended Lemon Drop into the prepared martini glasses and serve.

Lemon Simple Syrup: Combine the water and sugar in a small saucepan and bring to a boil. Simmer, while stirring, over low heat until the sugar dissolves. Cool to room temperature, add the lemon juice, and stir until completely combined. Transfer to a glass bottle and store in the refrigerator until use. Makes about 3 cups.

YOU'LL NEED:
√ 72 ounce Pitcher
√ Blade Assembly
√ Pitcher Lid

RULE THE KITC

CRÈME DE BANANA

SERVES 1

A great way to get your daily servings of fruit!

4 to 6 crushed ice cubes
1 banana, peeled
2 ounces light rum
2 ounces Crème de Banana
4 ounces pineapple juice
slice of fresh pineapple for garnish

Put the ice cubes into the bowl and add the remaining ingredients, except the garnish. Blend on ❸ until smooth. Pour into a chilled glass, garnish with the fresh pineapple and serve with a straw.

✳ TIP

To create a spectacular presentation with only two ingredients, shave 4 cups of ice in the *Ninja™ blender* and divide among 4 glasses. Pour straight shots of Crème de Banana over the ice and serve at once.

YOU'LL NEED:

✓ 40 ounce Bowl
✓ Blade Assembly
✓ Bowl Lid

HOT APPLE PIE ALA MODE

SERVES 2

An apple-licious treat for any season.

2 cups vanilla ice cream
1 cup crushed ice cubes
½ teaspoon ground cinnamon
½ teaspoon ground nutmeg
4 ounces vanilla vodka
4 ounces Calvados

Garnish
¼ cup superfine sugar
⅛ teaspoon ground cinnamon
Whipped cream

Place all ingredients, except the garnishes, into the pitcher and blend on ❸ until smooth. Combine the superfine sugar and cinnamon in a shallow saucer. Moisten the rims of two rocks glasses with calvados and dip the rim in the sugar-cinnamon mixture. Divide the drink between the glasses and top with whipped cream and a sprinkle of cinnamon-sugar.

TIP

Calvados is an apple brandy from Normandy, France, and is well-known for the distinctively rich and smooth apple flavor it imbues into food and drinks. It is well worth the investment to buy Calvados even if you are only going to use it sparingly along the rim of your cocktail glass.

YOU'LL NEED:

✓ 72 ounce Pitcher
✓ Blade Assembly
✓ Pitcher Lid

RULE THE KITC

CRUSHED PEPPERMINT SNOWFALL MARTINI

MAKES 2 SERVINGS

A festive drink, especially around the winter holidays.

1 cup peppermint candy, unwrapped
2 ounces good quality vodka
1½ ounces Peppermint Schnapps
1 ounce white chocolate liqueur
1 ounce white Crème de mint
2 ounces heavy cream

Place the peppermint candy into the pitcher and pulse on ❸ until finely crushed. Pour onto a shallow saucer and set aside. Clean and dry the blender.

Place all the remaining ingredients in the pitcher and pulse on ❶ until blended. Moisten the rim of each martini glass with Peppermint Schnapps and dip each in crushed peppermint. Fill the prepared glasses with the blended martini.

✳ TIP

Double or triple this recipe for a party. It is a beautiful drink to serve and a minty shot of liqueur on the tongue!

YOU'LL NEED:

✓ 72 ounce Pitcher
✓ Blade Assembly
✓ Pitcher Lid

THE KITCHEN®

JAMAICAN SCREWDRIVER

MAKES 4 SERVINGS

The added kick of rum turns this Screwdriver into a "Jamaican-style" pleasure!

6 ounces good quality vodka
4 ounces light rum
2 cups orange juice
1 cup pineapple juice
4 cups crushed ice cubes
4 orange slices for garnish

Place all the ingredients, except the orange slices, into the pitcher and blend on ❸ until smooth and frothy. Pour into tall chilled glasses and garnish with the orange slices.

✳ TIP

A traditional screwdriver cocktail is simply vodka and orange juice poured over ice, and has been hugely popular for several decades. This variation adds pineapple juice and light rum for more flavor and the frozen blend makes it perfect for brunch or breakfast on a weekend morning.

YOU'LL NEED:

✓ 72 ounce Pitcher
✓ Blade Assembly
✓ Pitcher Lid

RULE THE KITC

BUSHWACKER

MAKES 2 SERVINGS

Beware the Bushwacker! This cocktail really packs a punch, hence the name.

2 ounces dark rum
2 ounces Kahlua
2 ounces dark crème de cacao
2 ounces coconut liqueur
4 ounces heavy cream
2 cups crushed ice cubes

Garnish
Whipped cream
Ground nutmeg

Place all ingredients, except the whipped cream and nutmeg, into the pitcher and blend on ❸ until smooth. Pour into tall glasses and garnish with whipped cream and a sprinkle of nutmeg.

✳ TIP

Change this up by substituting cream of coconut for the coconut liqueur, amaretto for the Kahlua, or try using equal portions of dark and light rum. Every substitution creates an entirely new drink, worthy of tasting and testing among friends!

THE KITCHEN

YOU'LL NEED:

✓ 72 ounce Pitcher
✓ Blade Assembly
✓ Pitcher Lid

SOUTH PACIFIC SLUSH

MAKES 2 SERVINGS

You will be able to hear the ocean breeze blowing through the palm trees as you sip this delicious island sensation.

2 cups crushed ice cubes
4 ounces dark rum
4 ounces orange juice
2 ounces coconut milk
1 banana, peeled
2 tablespoons lime juice

Garnish
8 pineapple chunks
4 orange wedges, halved
2 thin wooden skewers
2 splashes grenadine

Place the ice cubes into the pitcher, add the remaining ingredients, except the garnish, and blend on ❸ until slushy-smooth.

Thread the pineapple chunks and orange wedges alternately onto skewers. Pour the drinks into tall, chilled glasses and garnish with the fruit skewers and a splash of grenadine.

YOU'LL NEED:

✓ 72 ounce Pitcher
✓ Blade Assembly
✓ Pitcher Lid

RULE THE KITC

ROASTED
TOMATO & OLIVE
BRUSCHETTA
P. 86

CHAPTER FOUR

Appetizers, Dips & Spreads

WARM DIJON CHICKEN SPREAD

SERVES 6 TO 8

Savory and filling, with tangy Dijon mustard throughout.

1 tablespoon soft butter
3 large slices yellow onion, separated into rings
½ cup mayonnaise (regular or lowfat)
¼ cup milk
1 tablespoon fresh Italian parsley, minced,
plus more for garnish
½ teaspoon salt
¼ teaspoon pepper
3 tablespoons Dijon mustard
2 cups cooked chicken, boneless and skinless
1 loaf French or thin sourdough bread,
sliced thinly and toasted

In a sauté pan, melt the butter over medium heat. Add the onion rings and sauté for 6 to 8 minutes, or until lightly caramelized. Remove from the heat and cool slightly.

Place the mayonnaise, milk, parsley, salt, pepper, mustard, and chicken in the pitcher and add the cooked onion. Blend on ❶ for 30 seconds, or until uniformly mixed. Use a spatula to clean the sides of the pitcher and blend again, if needed. Add a few drops of milk, if needed. Taste and adjust the seasonings to your liking. In a glass serving dish, briefly heat the chicken spread in the microwave oven for 30 seconds to 1 minute to warm the spread thoroughly. Garnish the spread with parsley and serve on the pieces of toasted bread.

YOU'LL NEED:

✓ 72 ounce Pitcher
✓ Blade Assembly
✓ Pitcher Lid

THE KITCHEN®

OLIVE TAPENADE BRUSCHETTA

SERVES 8

Toss together green and black olives with capers for an intriguing twist on bruschetta.

6 ounce can black olives, drained
4 ounce can green olives, drained
3 tablespoons capers, rinsed
1 clove garlic, peeled
1 tablespoon lemon juice
2 tablespoons extra-virgin olive oil
1 baguette French bread, sliced and toasted

Place the black and green olives in the pitcher and add the capers, garlic, lemon juice, and olive oil. Blend on ❶ until uniform, but not completely smooth. To serve, spread the olive tapenade on toasted slices of French bread.

 TIP

Tapenade is equally at home served on bread or mixed with tomatoes and served over pita chips as a Mediterranean salsa of sorts. The sharp piquant flavors accent almost any bread or cracker flavor.

YOU'LL NEED:

✓ 72 ounce Pitcher
✓ Blade Assembly
✓ Pitcher Lid

CREAM CHEESE FRUIT DIP
WITH STRAWBERRIES

MAKES ABOUT 2 CUPS OF FRUIT DIP

A summery appetizer or a dessert? You'll have to make this delicious decision.

2 tablespoons orange juice
8 ounces cream cheese (whipped or regular)
7 ounce jar marshmallow crème
1 teaspoon lemon zest, grated
3 cups fresh, ripe strawberries, hulled and cleaned

Pour the juice into the pitcher and add the cream cheese, marshmallow crème and lemon zest. Blend on ❸ until smooth, about 20 seconds. Use a spatula to clean the sides of the pitcher and blend again, if needed.

Spoon the fruit dip into a serving dish and serve with the strawberries on the side.

✳ TIP

Because this dip is sweet, yet cream cheese tangy, partner it with slices of pound cake or spread it on cinnamon toast for a new twist. After one taste, you'll find a million delicious variations of your own.

YOU'LL NEED:

✓ 72 ounce Pitcher
✓ Blade Assembly
✓ Pitcher Lid

HOT ARTICHOKE DIP
WITH SOURDOUGH ROUNDS

SERVES 8

A warm, melty artichoke dip that practically begs for soft sourdough bread. Enjoy with a glass of chilled chardonnay.

1 cup Rich & Creamy Mayonnaise (see p. 187)
4 ounce can marinated artichokes, reserve 2 tablespoons liquid
½ pound lowfat mozzarella cheese, cut into large pieces
½ cup Parmesan cheese, cut into pieces or grated
2 green onions, sliced
1 round sourdough bread, cut into 2-inch pieces

Preheat the oven to 350°F. Place the mayonnaise, artichokes with 2 tablespoons liquid, mozzarella cheese and Parmesan cheese in the pitcher. Blend on ❷ for 20 seconds. Use a spatula to clean the sides of the pitcher and blend again on ❷ until uniformly smooth. Spoon the dip into a heat-proof serving dish.

Bake the artichoke dip for 20 minutes or until heated through completely. Serve the dip with a wide knife for spreading on the sourdough bread.

❋TIP

If you like to prep in advance, place the prepared dip in a small slow cooker and cook on low heat for 4 hours. Stir just before serving.

YOU'LL NEED:

✓ 72 ounce Pitcher
✓ Blade Assembly
✓ Pitcher Lid

MINI CRAB CAKES WITH DILL SAUCE

SERVES 4

A smooth dill sauce accompanies each mini crab cake.

Dill Sauce

1 cup Rich & Creamy Mayonnaise (see p. 187)
2 tablespoons cream or milk
2 tablespoons fresh dill, chopped
2 tablespoons white onion, roughly cut
1 teaspoon lemon juice
½ teaspoon salt

Mini Crab Cakes

1 pound fresh crabmeat, picked through & cleaned
1 large egg, beaten
1 cup crushed saltine cracker crumbs
3 tablespoons Parmesan cheese
1 sprig fresh parsley
1 clove garlic, peeled
¼ small onion, peeled
½ teaspoon salt
vegetable oil for frying
parsley for garnish

Dill Sauce: Place all of the ingredients in the pitcher. Blend on ❸ until uniform. Remove and spoon into a small serving dish. Refrigerate until use.

Mini Crab Cakes: Place the crabmeat, egg, cracker crumbs, cheese, parsley, garlic, onion and salt in the pitcher. Blend on ❶ for 10 seconds. Use a spatula to clean the sides of the pitcher and blend again on ❶ until almost smooth.

Shape the crabmeat mixture into small, walnut-sized balls. Flatten slightly to form a small cake shape. In a large skillet, add enough vegetable oil to cover about ½-inch of the depth of the pan. Heat the oil to 350°F.

Carefully place the mini crab cakes in the oil to form a single layer. Fry for 1 minute; turn and fry for 1 to 2 minutes, or until cooked through. Remove from the oil with a slotted spoon and drain briefly on paper towels. Repeat with the remaining cakes.

Serve the cakes while hot with a small spoonful of the dill sauce on top of each. Add a small piece of parsley to finish the appetizer.

YOU'LL NEED:

✓ 72 ounce Pitcher
✓ Blade Assembly
✓ Pitcher Lid

CHILI CON QUESO
WITH TEX MEX SALSA

SERVES 6 TO 8

Yummy cheese dip with fresh salsa!

2 tablespoons butter
2 tablespoons flour
1 cup milk
4 cups cheddar cheese, grated
½ teaspoon salt
1 small yellow onion, quartered
½ green pepper, seeded
3 cloves garlic, peeled
1 jalapeño pepper, seeded

Tex Mex Salsa
2 ripe tomatoes, quartered
¼ small onion
½ jalapeño pepper, seeded
1 sprig fresh cilantro
salt and pepper to taste
tortilla chips

In a saucepan, heat the butter on medium heat. Stir and add the flour, cooking until smooth. Slowly add the milk as the mixture thickens. Add the cheese and stir well. Add salt to taste. Remove from the heat and cool slightly.

Place the yellow onion, green pepper, garlic and jalapeño pepper in the pitcher. Blend on ❶ just until chopped. Add the cheese sauce through the lid pour tab and blend again briefly on ❶. Pour into a serving dish and set aside.

To make the Tex Mex Salsa, place the tomatoes, onion, pepper, cilantro, salt and pepper in the pitcher and blend on ❶ just until chunky. To serve, spoon the queso over the chips and garnish with the salsa.

YOU'LL NEED:

✓ 72 ounce Pitcher
✓ Blade Assembly
✓ Pitcher Lid

THE KITCHEN®

BLUE CHEESE SLIDERS

SERVES 6 TO 12 AS APPETIZERS OR 4 AS A MAIN COURSE.

A hearty appetizer or casual entrée, these sliders marry grilled onions and a bold blue cheese spread for added oomph.

Blue Cheese Spread
1 cup sour cream (regular or lowfat)
1 cup mayonnaise (regular or lowfat)
4 ounces blue cheese, crumbled
1 clove garlic, peeled
2 green onions, chopped
pinch salt

Sliders
1½ pounds lean ground beef
½ teaspoon salt
½ teaspoon garlic salt
½ teaspoon black pepper
12 small rolls or buns, split horizontally, toasted
12 small pieces of lettuce
12 thin slices Roma tomatoes

Blue Cheese Spread: Combine all ingredients in the bowl. Blend on ❸ until smooth. Spoon into a bowl and refrigerate until use.

Sliders: In a large bowl, lightly toss together the beef, salt, garlic salt, and pepper. Form into small patties about the 1½ inches in diameter to form a total of 12 patties. Broil or grill each to your preference.

To assemble the sliders, place a small amount of the blue cheese spread on both sides of one roll. Top with a small piece of lettuce, a beef patty and a tomato slice. Cover with the remaining half roll.

YOU'LL NEED:

✓ 40 ounce Bowl
✓ Blade Assembly
✓ Bowl Lid

WHITE BEAN & SAGE SPREAD

SERVES 6

A simple spread with a hearty, savory impact!

14 ounce can cannelloni beans,
drained, 3 tablespoons liquid reserved
¼ cup extra-virgin olive oil
1 tablespoon fresh sage leaves
½ teaspoon salt
¼ teaspoon white pepper
¼ cup Parmesan cheese, grated
pita bread, torn into small pieces

Preheat the oven to 350°F. Place the beans and reserved liquid in the pitcher. Add the oil, sage leaves, salt, and pepper. Blend on ❷ for 20 seconds. Use a spatula to clean the sides of the pitcher and blend again on ❷ until mostly smooth throughout. Spoon the dip into a heatproof serving dish and cover with the Parmesan cheese.

Bake the spread for 20 minutes, or until piping hot. Offer the spread with the pita bread pieces.

TIP

Although this tastes very rich and smooth, your guests will be surprised to learn that the ingredients are a good-for-you combination of protein-rich beans, olive oil and cheese. Serve with whole wheat crackers or any other sturdy cracker or bread.

YOU'LL NEED:

✓ 72 ounce Pitcher
✓ Blade Assembly
✓ Pitcher Lid

GRILLED SHRIMP
WITH FRESH PEACH SALSA

SERVES 4

Grilled shrimp has a slightly sweet and mild flavor, perfectly accentuated by the tangy, spicy peach salsa.

Fresh Peach Salsa
2 fresh, ripe peaches, pitted and peeled
½ fresh mango, peeled
¼ fresh pineapple, peeled
2 sprigs fresh cilantro
¼ small white onion, peeled

Grilled Shrimp
1 tablespoon lemon juice
1 clove garlic, minced
2 tablespoons soy sauce
¼ cup vegetable oil
1 pound fresh shrimp, peeled, tails removed
cilantro for garnish

Fresh Peach Salsa: Place all ingredients into the pitcher and pulse on **❶** until chunky, about 15 seconds. Remove and refrigerate until ready to use.

Grilled Shrimp: Place the lemon juice, garlic, soy sauce and oil in a plastic self-sealing bag. Add the shrimp and refrigerate for 1 hour. Thread the shrimp onto wooden or metal skewers and grill over medium heat for 2 minutes on each side, or until cooked through. Shrimp are done when they turn opaque and pink.

Serve the shrimp skewers on small plates accompanied by the salsa. Garnish with additional cilantro if desired.

YOU'LL NEED:

✓ 72 ounce Pitcher
✓ Blade Assembly
✓ Pitcher Lid

ROASTED TOMATO & OLIVE BRUSCHETTA

MAKES ABOUT 12 SERVINGS

Roasting brings out such sweet tomato flavors and, with the addition of garlic and basil, you can't go wrong with this inviting appetizer! Use lightly toasted French bread or sourdough baguette rounds for the base.

4 medium tomatoes, cored and quartered
2 tablespoons extra-virgin olive oil
salt and pepper to taste
1 clove garlic, peeled
¼ cup black olives, pitted
1 teaspoon fresh basil
French bread rounds, lightly toasted

Place the tomatoes on a baking sheet and toss with the oil. Sprinkle with salt and pepper. Bake at 350°F for 30 to 40 minutes, or until very soft and tender. Remove and cool slightly.

Place the cooled tomatoes in the bowl and add the garlic, olives and basil. Add a few drops of oil if the mixture looks dry. Pulse on ❶ for just a few seconds, or long enough to roughly chop the vegetables together. Don't over-blend.

YOU'LL NEED:

✓ 40 ounce Bowl
✓ Blade Assembly
✓ Bowl Lid

PITA CHIPS WITH TANGY TAHINI SPREAD

MAKES ABOUT 1¾ CUPS

Tahini is a roasted sesame seed paste that can be found in the Ethnic Foods aisle of most grocery stores. Tahini spread is the secret behind many excellent Middle Eastern dips, spreads and salads. When you feel lazy, pour some of this spread into a shallow bowl and serve as a dipping sauce for pita bread – it's that easy!

¼ cup canola oil
¼ cup water
¼ cup sesame tahini
2 tablespoons apple cider vinegar
4 teaspoons soy sauce
2 tablespoons toasted sesame oil
1 tablespoon fresh lemon juice
2 cloves garlic, peeled
1 tablespoon fresh parsley, chopped
2 chives, cleaned and chopped in quarters
½ teaspoon salt
½ teaspoon freshly ground black pepper
4 cups pita chips

Place all ingredients into the pitcher and blend on ❶ until smooth. Taste and adjust the flavors and consistency, adding more soy sauce or vinegar for stronger flavor, or a little water to thin if it becomes too thick. Serve with the pita chips.

YOU'LL NEED:

✓ 72 ounce Pitcher
✓ Blade Assembly
✓ Pitcher Lid

RULE THE KITC

CHICKEN
TORTILLA SOUP
P. 93

CHAPTER FIVE
Soups, Bisque & Sauces

GAZPACHO

MAKES 4 TO 6 SERVINGS

This age-old soup from Spain originally took hours to make using a mortar and pestle. With the *Ninja™Blender*, your soup is finished in just a few minutes! For a traditional version that includes day-old French bread, soak the bread in water and squeeze out the excess. Blend with the vegetables to create a heavier soup.

1 large cucumber, peeled and cut into pieces
1 red bell pepper, cored, seeded, and quartered
1 green bell pepper, cored, seeded, and quartered
4 ripe tomatoes, cored and quartered
1 red onion, peeled and quartered
4 cloves garlic, peeled
½ bunch flat leaf parsley, stemmed
1½ cups tomato juice
2 tablespoons red wine vinegar
2 tablespoons olive oil, (optional)
2 teaspoons ground paprika
½ teaspoon salt
½ teaspoon freshly ground black pepper

Place the cucumber, bell peppers, tomatoes, onion, garlic and parsley into the pitcher and pulse until the vegetables are coarsely chopped. Transfer half of the vegetable mixture into a large mixing bowl. Add the remaining ingredients to the pitcher and blend on ❷ until smooth. Add the smooth vegetable mixture to the mixing bowl, stirring well to incorporate all ingredients.

Cover tightly and refrigerate for at least 2 hours or until well-chilled. The longer the soup sits, the more flavor it develops. Taste and adjust seasonings as desired. Serve in chilled bowls with sliced cucumber, bell peppers, and chopped parsley as fresh summer croutons.

YOU'LL NEED:

✓ **72 ounce Pitcher**
✓ **Blade Assembly**
✓ **Pitcher Lid**

CREAMY AVOCADO SOUP

MAKES 4 TO 6 SERVINGS

With all the flavors of guacamole, this soup is the perfect starter for a festive Mexican dinner.

2 large ripe avocados, peeled, pitted and quartered
8 green onions, cleaned
2 cups chicken stock, warmed (vegetable stock may be used if desired)
2 tablespoons fresh lime juice
2 tablespoons fresh cilantro, chopped
½ teaspoon salt
¾ teaspoon cumin or more to taste
½ teaspoon red chile powder or more to taste
1 cup heavy cream
4 to 6 sprigs cilantro for garnish

Place the avocado, green onions, chicken stock, lime juice, chopped cilantro, salt, cumin, and red chile powder into the pitcher and blend on **2** until just mixed. Add the heavy cream and blend again until the soup is just smooth. Do not over-blend. Taste and adjust the seasonings as desired.

Serve at room temperature or cover and refrigerate for at least 2 hours to serve chilled. Garnish with a sprig of cilantro before serving.

YOU'LL NEED:

✓ 72 ounce Pitcher
✓ Blade Assembly
✓ Pitcher Lid

RULE THE KITCHE

SUMMER STRAWBERRY MINT SOUP

MAKES 4 SERVINGS

Pack this chilled soup in a thermos for a special addition to any picnic.

2 cups water
4 cups fresh strawberries, stemmed and hulled (or use frozen, thawed strawberries)
2 tablespoons superfine white sugar
1 tablespoon fresh lime juice
½ cup good quality chardonnay
6 large mint leaves, chopped (about 4 tablespoons)

Garnish
4 sprigs of mint for garnish
½ cup Greek yogurt for garnish

Place all ingredients, except the garnishes, into the pitcher and blend on ❶ until smooth. Cover and refrigerate for 2 hours to chill. (If you prefer, serve at room temperature.) Serve in bowls with a dollop of yogurt and garnish with a mint sprig.

✳ TIP

You can't imagine how wonderful this chilled soup is on a hot summer day! Add a meal of cooked cold shrimp or crab over greens dressed with Lemon Garlic Aioli (p. 186), and you have a meal fit for royalty.

YOU'LL NEED:

✓ **72 ounce Pitcher**
✓ **Blade Assembly**
✓ **Pitcher Lid**

CHICKEN TORTILLA SOUP

MAKES 4 TO 6 SERVINGS

A yummy soup with rich flavor and texture!

1 large white onion, peeled and quartered
3 cloves garlic, peeled
4 jalapeño peppers, seeded
1 red bell pepper, cored and seeded
2 teaspoons extra-virgin olive oil
8 ounce can crushed tomatoes
3 tablespoons fresh cilantro, chopped
(1 tablespoon is reserved for garnish)
4 to 6 cups chicken stock
2 tablespoons fresh lime juice
1 teaspoon ground cumin
½ teaspoon salt (or to taste)
1 teaspoon freshly ground black pepper
4 6-inch corn tortillas
2 cups chicken, cooked and shredded
1 avocado, pitted, peeled, and diced
1 cup Jack cheese, shredded
2 cups tortilla chips, crumbled
1 lime, cut into wedges

Place the onion, garlic, peppers and red pepper in the pitcher and pulse on ❶ until chopped. Heat the oil in a stockpot over medium heat. Add the chopped vegetables, tomatoes, and 2 tablespoons of cilantro. Sauté and stir for about 5 minutes, or until the vegetables soften. Add the chicken stock, juice, cumin, salt and pepper. Reduce the heat and simmer until the vegetables are tender, about 15 minutes.

Place two-thirds of the soup into the pitcher. Briefly heat the corn tortillas in a dry skillet over medium heat just until softened. Tear the tortillas into pieces, add to the pitcher and blend on ❷ until the mixture is fairly smooth and thick. Pour the blended soup back into the stockpot, stirring well to incorporate.

Divide the shredded chicken between 4 soup bowls. Ladle the hot soup into the bowls and top with diced avocado, Jack cheese and crumbled tortilla strips. Garnish the soup with the remaining chopped cilantro and lime wedges.

YOU'LL NEED:

✓ 72 ounce Pitcher
✓ Blade Assembly
✓ Pitcher Lid

RULE THE KITCHE

CLASSIC LOBSTER BISQUE

SERVES 4

Lobster Bisque is the height of elegance! Use your *Ninja™ Blender* to cut your prep time and eliminate major mistakes.

1 medium carrot, peeled and roughly chopped
1 medium onion, peeled and roughly chopped
1 inside stalk celery, peeled, strings removed and roughly chopped
½ cup unsalted butter, divided
2 uncooked lobster tails, with shells
¼ cup pale dry sherry or brandy
¼ cup dry white wine
6 cups fish stock
1 tablespoon tomato paste
1 bay leaf
6 sprigs fresh parsley
2 stems fresh thyme
3 tablespoons white flour
1 cup heavy cream
salt and white pepper to taste
brandy as garnish

Place the carrot, onion and celery into the pitcher and blend on ❷ until the vegetables are minced. In a heavy-bottomed soup pot, melt half the butter over medium-low heat and add the carrots, onion, celery and the lobster tails in shells. Sauté 3 to 4 minutes. Add the sherry, wine, fish stock, tomato paste and herbs and simmer the stock for 30 to 40 minutes. Remove the lobsters from the stock, remove the meat from the shells and cut into large chunks, setting aside. Strain the stock through a sieve.

In a large saucepan over medium heat, melt the remaining butter. Whisk in the flour, stirring to make a roux. Steadily, whisk in the strained lobster stock, until smoothly blended.

Transfer the soup into the pitcher, in batches as needed, and blend on ❷ until smooth. Return the soup to the stockpot, add the lobster and cream and simmer, stirring frequently for 10 minutes. Adjust the seasonings, if desired. To serve, pour the soup into bowls and add a splash of brandy on top. Store any leftovers in the refrigerator.

YOU'LL NEED:

✓ 72 ounce Pitcher
✓ Blade Assembly
✓ Pitcher Lid

CREAM OF BROCCOLI SOUP

SERVES 6 TO 8

This delectable soup uses potatoes to thicken the delicious stock, cutting out much of the usual cream and creating a healthier version of a favorite comfort food.

2 tablespoons butter
1 tablespoon extra-virgin olive oil
1 medium shallot, peeled and chopped
1 large russet potato, peeled and diced
1 cup water
1 cup chicken stock
1 medium head of broccoli, cut into florets, stock peeled and chunked
½ teaspoon salt
½ teaspoon white pepper
¾ cup heavy cream
¼ teaspoon ground nutmeg

Heat the butter and oil over medium-low heat in a medium saucepan; add the shallot, cover and sweat, stirring occasionally, until softened. Add the diced potato, water and chicken stock. Increase the heat and bring just to a boil. Reduce the heat to medium-low and simmer, stirring occasionally for 8 minutes. Add the broccoli, salt, and pepper and simmer for an additional 5 to 6 minutes, depending on the size of dice, until the potatoes and broccoli are tender.

Ladle the soup in batches, into the pitcher and blend on ❷ until very smooth. Add the cream and nutmeg and pulse to incorporate. Pour the soup back into the saucepan and cook over medium heat to thicken slightly. Taste and adjust the seasonings before serving.

YOU'LL NEED:

✓ 72 ounce Pitcher
✓ Blade Assembly
✓ Pitcher Lid

RULE THE KITCHEN

POTATO & CORN CHOWDER

MAKES 6 TO 8 SERVINGS

This "stick to your ribs," hearty soup is sure to become a family favorite. The green chile adds that mildly spicy taste of the Southwest.

4 slices apple-wood smoked bacon
1 large onion, peeled and chopped
1 green bell pepper, cored, seeded and chopped
4 medium russet potatoes, peeled and diced
2 cups chicken stock
½ teaspoon freshly ground black pepper
2 cups fresh or frozen corn kernels
2 cups whole milk
4 ounce can chopped New Mexican green chilies
1 cup heavy cream
pinch salt (optional)
4 tablespoons fresh chives, minced

Cook the bacon in a stockpot over medium-high heat until crisp. Drain on paper towels and crumble when cooled. Pour off all but about 3 tablespoons of the bacon drippings, re-heat and add the onion, green pepper and potatoes. Stir to coat and sauté for 3 to 4 minutes. Add the chicken stock and pepper and reduce the heat to medium-low. Cook, stirring occasionally, for 8 minutes.

While the potatoes are cooking, place 1 cup of corn and 1 cup of milk into the pitcher and blend on ② until roughly uniform. Add the blended mixture to the potatoes, along with the remaining corn, milk and the green chile. Continue cooking until the corn and potatoes are tender.

Stir in the heavy cream and simmer for a few additional minutes. Taste and adjust the seasonings as desired. Serve in soup bowls garnished with the chives and generous amounts of crumbled bacon.

YOU'LL NEED:

✓ **72 ounce Pitcher**
✓ **Blade Assembly**
✓ **Pitcher Lid**

FRESH TOMATO BASIL SOUP

MAKES 4 SERVINGS

In the summer months, this is a great way to use tomatoes ripening in your garden. Run them through a food mill to remove skin and seeds, but retain all that powerful, antioxidant juice.

1 teaspoon extra-virgin olive oil
1 small yellow onion, peeled and chopped
1 medium shallot, peeled and chopped
3 medium tomatoes, seeded and chopped
(or 28 ounce can whole tomatoes)
1½ cups vegetable stock
1 cup heavy cream
½ teaspoon salt
½ teaspoon white pepper
1 teaspoon fresh thyme leaves
½ cup packed fresh basil
6 large fresh basil leaves, stacked, rolled lengthwise and thinly sliced (chiffonade), for garnish

Heat the oil in a large stockpot over medium-low heat. Add the onion and shallots, cover the pan and sweat, stirring occasionally, until softened, but not browned. Add the tomatoes, vegetable stock, cream, salt, pepper, and thyme and simmer for 10 minutes, stirring occasionally. Stir in the ½ cup basil.

Transfer the soup, in batches, to the pitcher and blend on ❷ until smooth. Return the soup to the stockpot to re-heat over low heat. Do not allow the soup to boil. Taste and adjust the seasonings as desired. Serve in soup bowls with a sprinkling of the chiffonade basil.

YOU'LL NEED:

✓ **72 ounce Pitcher**
✓ **Blade Assembly**
✓ **Pitcher Lid**

WINTER VEGETABLE BEAN SOUP

SERVES 6 TO 8

A good way to use up vegetables hanging around in your refrigerator, this hearty soup will warm your family on a cold winter's eve. Serve with crusty French bread & butter.

2 cloves garlic, peeled
½ cup flat leaf Italian parsley, roughly cut
¼ cup Parmesan cheese, freshly grated
¼ cup + 2 tablespoons extra-virgin olive oil
2 medium russet potatoes, peeled and cut into 1 inch pieces
2 medium carrots, peeled and cut into 1 inch pieces
2 ribs celery, with leaves, strings removed, cut into 1 inch pieces
2 leeks, white and light green parts only, cleaned well and sliced
6 to 8 cups vegetable stock
1 teaspoon salt
1 teaspoon freshly ground black pepper
½ teaspoon crushed red pepper flakes
28 ounce can whole peeled tomatoes with juice
2 medium zucchini, cut into 1 inch pieces
15 ounce can white kidney beans, drained
¾ cup Parmesan cheese rinds

Place garlic, parsley, grated Parmesan cheese and ¼ cup olive oil into the pitcher and blend on ❷ until almost pureed. Set aside.

In a large stockpot, heat 2 tablespoons olive oil over medium heat. Add the potatoes, carrots, celery and leeks and sauté, stirring occasionally, for 4 to 5 minutes. Add the vegetable stock, salt, black pepper, red pepper flakes, and canned tomatoes with juice. Reduce the heat to medium-low and simmer for an additional 10 to 15 minutes, until the vegetables are tender.

Add the zucchini, beans, Parmesan cheese rinds, and herb mixture from the blender and simmer for an additional 4 to 6 minutes to cook the zucchini and combine the flavors. Taste and add salt and pepper before serving, if desired.

YOU'LL NEED:

✓ **72 ounce Pitcher**
✓ **Blade Assembly**
✓ **Pitcher Lid**

RULE THE KITCHE

VICHYSSOISE

SERVES 4 TO 6

Leeks are grown in sandy soil and are notoriously difficult to clean. The best way is to slice off one-fourth inch of the root end and cut lengthwise only through the white and light green part, leaving the dark green leaves intact. Turn the leek a quarter turn and repeat, cutting the leek into quarters lengthwise, still leaving the dark green leaves intact. Rinse white and light green section of leek under cool running water, fanning them apart to expose the dirt and sand.

2 large leeks, white part only, cleaned well
2 medium russet potatoes, peeled and diced
2 cups water
2 cups chicken stock
½ teaspoon salt
½ teaspoon white pepper
1 cup heavy cream
1 tablespoon fresh chives, minced

In a heavy bottomed stockpot, bring the leeks, potatoes, water, chicken stock, salt and pepper to a boil. Partially cover the pan and reduce to a simmer for 20 to 30 minutes, or until the potatoes and leeks are tender.

Stir in the heavy cream and transfer the soup, in batches, to the pitcher. Blend on ❷ until smooth. Taste and adjust the seasonings as desired. Refrigerate the soup for at least 2 hours to serve chilled, or return the soup to the stockpot and heat over medium-low to serve warm. Garnish with minced chives.

YOU'LL NEED:

✓ **72 ounce Pitcher**
✓ **Blade Assembly**
✓ **Pitcher Lid**

CLASSIC HOLLANDAISE SAUCE

MAKE ABOUT ¾ CUP

Using the *Ninja™Blender* Pitcher takes care of the problem of separation and turns this sometimes troublesome preparation into the easiest sauce ever. A lovely Hollandaise sauce always adds a touch of sophistication to a vegetable dish or your Sunday eggs. Enjoy!

3 large egg yolks
1 teaspoon fresh lemon juice
pinch dry mustard
pinch cayenne pepper
pinch salt
2 cups unsalted butter
a few tablespoons of hot water to thin as necessary

Place the egg yolks, lemon juice, mustard, cayenne pepper and salt in the pitcher and blend on ❶ until combined, cleaning the sides of the blender with a spatula if needed.

In a small sauce pan, melt the butter, skimming the foam off the top. Discard the foam. Gently pour the clarified butter off of the milk solids that have settled in the bottom of the pan. With the blender running on ❷, slowly pour the hot melted butter, in a thin stream, through the top pour tab, into the egg mixture. As the sauce thickens, continue blending until the sauce is smooth and as thin as you prefer. Add water as necessary, a tablespoon at a time, to prevent the Hollandaise Sauce from over-thickening. Serve at once or keep warm over a pan of hot water.

YOU'LL NEED:

✓ **72 ounce Pitcher**
✓ **Blade Assembly**
✓ **Pitcher Lid**

RULE THE KITCHE

BASIL PESTO

MAKES ABOUT 2 CUPS

A versatile sauce to have on hand in the fridge or freezer. Toss with pasta, use as a marinade or a sauce for fish or chicken. Substitute spinach, roasted red pepper or broccoli for a twist on this classic.

½ cup toasted pine nuts
2 large cloves garlic, peeled
4 cups tightly packed fresh basil leaves
½ cup freshly grated Parmesan cheese
½ teaspoon salt
½ teaspoon freshly ground black pepper
½ to ¾ cup extra virgin olive oil

Place all of the ingredients, except the olive oil, into the pitcher and blend on **2** until combined, but still containing some texture.

With the blender running on **2**, drizzle the olive oil through the top pour tab and blend until smooth. Use right away or store in the refrigerator for up to 4 days until use.

TIP

It's ridiculously easy to make pesto and it's also tremendously easy to grow your own basil. Try planting a small herb garden and make basil your centerpiece. Basil will grow in full sun with a little bit of water and loving care – not much else is needed for success. Vacuum bag and freeze the basil pesto in small portions for quick and easy use all year long.

YOU'LL NEED:

✓ **72 ounce Pitcher**
✓ **Blade Assembly**
✓ **Pitcher Lid**

HOMEMADE PIZZA SAUCE

MAKES ABOUT 1¾ CUPS, OR ENOUGH FOR 2 PIZZAS

Fresh pizza dough is so easy – check it out on page 110. All you need to add is this delightfully fresh sauce. Use this along with your favorite toppings for the perfect addition to a fun family movie night.

6 ounce can tomato paste

1 cup warm water

2 cloves garlic, peeled

6 large leaves fresh basil

½ teaspoon onion powder

¼ teaspoon dried oregano

¼ teaspoon dried marjoram

½ teaspoon freshly ground black pepper

½ teaspoon salt

½ teaspoon dried red pepper flakes

Place all of the ingredients in the bowl and blend on ❷ until thoroughly combined. Adjust the seasonings to your taste and add a pinch of sugar if you want to balance the acidity of the tomatoes.

✳TIP

Make a double-batch of this sauce and freeze half for another night. Pair it with hot pasta and a grating of fresh Parmesan, pour it over chicken breasts and bake with mozzarella cheese, the list of uses is endless!

YOU'LL NEED:

✓ 40 ounce Bowl

✓ Blade Assembly

✓ Bowl Lid

RULE THE KITCHEN

SOUTH AMERICAN CHIMICHURRI SAUCE

MAKES 1 TO 1½ CUPS

There are many versions of this classic South American accompaniment for grilled meats. This recipe is a good, solid place to start using your imagination, as you add ingredients to your taste.

1 bunch fresh parsley, cleaned, large stems removed
10 large cloves garlic, peeled
1 teaspoon salt
1 cup extra-virgin olive oil

Optional ingredients:
1 small white onion, peeled and quartered
½ cup white wine vinegar
½ teaspoon fresh ground pepper
1 teaspoon fresh basil, thyme or oregano or a mixture of any favorite herbs

Place the parsley, garlic, salt and oil (and optional ingredients) into the bowl and blend on **1** until finely chopped. Serve right away or store in a covered glass dish in the refrigerator for several days.

TIP

Chimichurri Sauce is more like a pesto with a hefty garlic flavor than it is a sauce and it has become increasing popular all over the world. Try it on tender lamb chops, beef kebabs, or any simple cut of beef, pork, or chicken.

YOU'LL NEED:

✓ **40 ounce Bowl**
✓ **Blade Assembly**
✓ **Bowl Lid**

SIMPLE RED RASPBERRY SAUCE

MAKES ABOUT 2 CUPS

A straight-forward sauce that stands alone or works well with the addition of other flavors such as vanilla or lemon. Buy raspberries in season when they are reasonably priced. This sauce freezes well for up to six months.

2 cups fresh or frozen raspberries
3 tablespoons raspberry jam
1 teaspoon raspberry liqueur

Place all ingredients into the pitcher and blend on ❷ until smooth. Add water for a thinner consistency, if needed. Strain to use in a thin sauce or use as is for a sauce with more texture and a dense consistency.

TIP

If you want to go wild, combine the Raspberry Sauce with red chilies and use as a sauce for grilling meat – it packs a flavorful punch!

YOU'LL NEED:

√ **72 ounce Pitcher**
√ **Blade Assembly**
√ **Pitcher Lid**

RULE THE KITCHE

CHIPOTLE TARTAR SAUCE

MAKES 1½ CUPS

Try this tangy twist on the traditional Tartar Sauce. Especially tasty with crunchy fried calamari or onion rings.

1 cup regular or lowfat mayonnaise
2 small chipotle peppers
¼ cup sweet pickle, diced
1 teaspoon juice from canned chipotles
2 teaspoons whole grain mustard
2 tablespoon white wine vinegar
1 teaspoon freshly ground black pepper
½ teaspoon salt

Place all of the ingredients into the pitcher and pulse on ❶ until the pickles are finely chopped and the tartar sauce is well blended, but not pureed. Transfer to a serving bowl or cover and store in the refrigerator.

✳ TIP

A Chipotle pepper is a ripe, smoked jalapeño pepper that offers rich, smoked and very spicy flavors. A little goes a long way, particularly when you also use the adobo sauce packed with chipotles in cans.

YOU'LL NEED:

✓ 72 ounce Pitcher
✓ Blade Assembly
✓ Pitcher Lid

PEANUT DIPPING SAUCE

MAKES 1½ CUPS

This sauce is a snap to prepare and can be used with just about any vegetable or chicken dish as a way to enliven your meal. If your kids like peanut butter, they will eat just about anything dipped in this sauce.

½ cup hot water
½ cup crunchy peanut butter
⅓ cup Hoisen sauce (or substitute soy sauce)
1 tablespoon Asian red chili paste
1 tablespoon fresh lime juice

Place all of the ingredients into the bowl and blend on 2 until completely combined. Taste and the adjust flavors and consistency to your liking.

TIP

This sauce also makes a delicious base for chicken lettuce wraps. Mince cooked chicken on 1, add 3 to 4 tablespoons of this sauce, and wrap in crisp lettuce leaves for a wonderful appetizer or snack.

YOU'LL NEED:

✓ 40 ounce Bowl
✓ Blade Assembly
✓ Bowl Lid

RULE THE KITCHEN

PECAN
CINNAMON
ROLLS
P. 119

CHAPTER SIX
Breads & Bakery Goods

EASY PIZZA DOUGH

MAKES 1 PIZZA CRUST

So incredibly easy when you make it in your *Ninja™Blender!* Start with this basic dough to make pizza crust, foccacia bread, calzones, rolls and bread sticks.

¼ ounce pkg. dry active yeast
1 teaspoon salt
1 tablespoon sugar
⅔ cup water, warmed to 110-115°F
¼ cup canola oil (substitute olive oil)
2 cups all-purpose flour

Place the yeast, salt, sugar and water in the bowl. Pulse on ① for 10 seconds. Add the oil and flour, 1 cup at a time, pulsing on ① until the dough is smooth and no lumps remain. Transfer the dough to a lightly-oiled bowl and cover. Let rise for about 1 hour.

If you are making high-rise pizza dough, punch down the dough and let rise again for 45 minutes. If not, eliminate the second rising and spread the dough onto a pizza pan or baking sheet that has been lightly coated with cooking spray.

Add sauce and toppings as preferred and bake at 425°F for 25-30 minutes, or until the crust is lightly browned and the toppings and cheese are hot.

YOU'LL NEED:

✓ 40 ounce Bowl
✓ Dough Blade
✓ Bowl Lid

BUTTERMILK BREAD

MAKES 1 GOLDEN LOAF

Offering a yeasty, homemade aroma and melt-in-your-mouth flavor, this bread doesn't disappoint!

¼ oz. pkg dry active yeast
¼ cup water, warmed to 110-115°F
2 tablespoons sugar
½ cup lowfat buttermilk
1 teaspoon salt
¼ cup vegetable oil
1 large egg, beaten
3¼ cups all-purpose flour

Place the yeast and warm water in a small bowl and stir well until the yeast is dissolved. Add the sugar and stir again. Let stand for about 5 minutes.

Place the buttermilk, salt, oil, egg and yeast mixture in the bowl and blend on ① for about 20 seconds. Add 1 cup of flour and blend on ① until the flour is incorporated. Use a spatula to clean the sides of the bowl. Add 1 cup of flour and blend again on ① until the dough is smooth. Clean the sides of the bowl. Add the remaining flour and pulse on ① until a smooth ball forms. Use a spatula to clean the sides of the dough bowl and continue pulsing on ① for 2 minutes, or until the ball of dough is very smooth and elastic.

Place the dough in a lightly-oiled bowl, cover, and let rise for 60 minutes, or until doubled in size. Prepare a 9-inch by 5-inch loaf pan by lightly coating with cooking spray. Form the dough into a loaf shape and place in the loaf pan. Cover and let rise again for 45 minutes, or until doubled in size again.

Bake at 375°F for 35 to 40 minutes, or until the bread is golden brown. Cool on a wire rack before slicing.

YOU'LL NEED:

✓ 40 ounce Bowl
✓ Dough Blade
✓ Bowl Lid

RULE THE KITCHEN

WHOLE GRAIN COWBOY BREAD

MAKES 1 LOAF

Saddle up and enjoy the texture and flavors of this satisfying bread!

¼ cup yellow corn meal
¼ cup dark brown sugar, packed
1 teaspoon salt
1 cup water, heated to boiling temperature
2 tablespoons canola oil
¼ ounce pkg. dry active yeast
¼ cup water, warmed to 110-115°F
⅓ cup whole wheat flour
¼ cup rye flour
2½ to 3 cups white flour

Place the corn meal, sugar, salt, boiling water, and oil in the bowl and blend on ① for about 10 seconds. Remove from the bowl and set aside. Let cool completely, about 30 minutes.

In a small bowl, dissolve the yeast in the warm water and stir well. Pour into the bowl and add the cooled corn meal mixture. Add the whole wheat flour and the rye flour and blend on ① until smooth. Use a spatula to clean the sides of the bowl. Add 1 cup of the white flour and blend again on ① until the dough is smooth and well-combined. Clean the sides of the bowl. Add the remaining flour as needed and pulse for 2 minutes on ① until the dough is very smooth and elastic.

Form the dough into a round and place in a mixing bowl that has been lightly coated with cooking spray. Cover and let rise for 50 to 60 minutes, or until doubled. Punch down the dough and let rest for 5 minutes. Lightly coat a 9-inch by 5-inch loaf pan with cooking spray and shape the dough to fit into the pan. Cover and let rise for 30 to 45 minutes, or until doubled.

Preheat the oven to 375°F. Bake the bread for 35 to 45 minutes, or until the top is golden and the bread sounds hollow when tapped.

YOU'LL NEED:

✓ 40 ounce Bowl
✓ Dough Blade
✓ Bowl Lid

PARMESAN & DILL BISCUITS

SERVES 6 TO 8

Biscuits often highlight the sweeter side of breads and are served with honey or jam, however these savory dill and Parmesan cheese biscuits are less sweet and perfectly suited to accompany beef or chicken.

¾ cup lowfat milk
1 teaspoon salt
¼ cup vegetable shortening
2 cups all-purpose flour
1 tablespoon baking powder
2 tablespoons Parmesan cheese, grated
1 tablespoon fresh dill, minced

Place the milk, salt and shortening in the bowl and blend until smooth. Add 1 cup of the flour and blend on ❶ until smooth. Clean the sides of the bowl with a spatula and add the remaining 1 cup flour, baking powder, cheese and dill. Pulse on ❶ for 30 seconds. Clean the sides of the bowl and pulse briefly again, just until the ingredients are incorporated.

Place the biscuit dough on a lightly floured board and gently round up. Pat the dough lightly with your hands into ½-inch thickness. Do not overwork the dough. Use a biscuit cutter to cut 12 to 16 biscuits. Gather the leftover dough together (without kneading) and cut additional biscuits.

Lightly coat a 9-inch x 9-inch baking pan with cooking spray and place the biscuits in the pan. The biscuits should touch each other and have little space between. Bake at 450°F for 10 to 12 minutes, or until fluffy and cooked through.

YOU'LL NEED:

✓ **40 ounce Bowl**
✓ **Dough Blade**
✓ **Bowl Lid**

RULE THE KITCHE

ITALIAN BREADSTICK TWISTS

MAKES 32 BREAD STICKS

Use any combination of spices on these breadsticks – you can't go wrong with any savory, zesty or spicy pairing.

¾ cup lowfat milk
1 tablespoon sugar
1 teaspoon salt
2 tablespoons vegetable oil
¼ oz. pkg. dry active yeast
¼ cup water, warmed to 115°F
3 to 3½ cups all-purpose flour
1 egg white
1 tablespoon water
3 tablespoons kosher salt
1 tablespoon cracked black pepper
1 tablespoon sesame seeds
1 tablespoon poppy seeds

Place the milk, sugar, salt and oil in the bowl and blend on ① for 10 seconds. Dissolve the yeast in the warm water and stir well. Add the yeast mixture to the bowl. Add 1 cup of the flour to the bowl and blend on ①

until the dough is smooth. Clean the sides of the bowl with a plastic spatula and add 1 cup of flour. Blend on ① until smooth. Clean the sides of the bowl again. Add the remaining flour as needed and pulse on ① for about 2 minutes, cleaning the sides of the bowl as needed.

Turn the dough into a lightly oiled bowl and cover. Let rise until doubled, about 45 to 60 minutes.

Place the dough on a lightly floured board and roll into a 16-inch by 6-inch rectangle. From the widest side, cut ½-inch wide strips. Twist each strip by hand and place on a baking sheet that has been coated with cooking spray. Cover and let rise for 30 to 45 minutes.

In a small bowl, combine the egg white and water. Brush onto each breadstick. Scatter the salt, pepper and seeds over the breadsticks before baking. Bake at 400°F for 10 to 15 minutes. Cool slightly on a wire rack.

YOU'LL NEED:

✓ 40 ounce Bowl
✓ Dough Blade
✓ Bowl Lid

APRICOT & DATE MUFFINS

MAKES 12 MUFFINS

Made with dried dates and apricots, these muffins are naturally sweet and contain only 2 tablespoons of sugar! Add a little whipped butter for a brunch specialty.

1 cup dates
½ cup dried apricots
¾ cup milk
1 large egg
½ cup vegetable shortening
2 tablespoons sugar
2 cups all-purpose flour
2½ teaspoons baking powder
1 teaspoon salt

Place the dates and apricots in the bowl and pulse on ❶ to uniformly chop. Remove and set aside.

Place the milk, egg and shortening in the bowl and add the sugar. Blend on ❶ until well-combined. Add 1 cup of the flour, the powder and the salt and blend on ❶ for about 10 seconds. Clean the sides of the bowl with a spatula and add the remaining flour. Blend on ❶ for 10 seconds. Add the date/apricot mixture and pulse on ❶ until the dried fruit is incorporated throughout.

Prepare a 12-cup muffin tin by generously coating each cup with shortening or using foil liners. Scoop a large tablespoon of batter into each of the cups and divide the remaining batter evenly among all the cups.

Bake at 400°F for 25 minutes, or until baked through.

YOU'LL NEED:

✓ **40 ounce Bowl**
✓ **Dough Paddle**
✓ **Bowl Lid**

RULE THE KITCHEN

OVERNIGHT DINNER ROLLS

MAKES 12 TO 18 ROLLS

The aroma of rich, yeasty dinner rolls in the oven will bring the entire household to the table in a flash. Expect these rolls to disappear quickly.

¼ ounce pkg active dry yeast
¼ cup warm water (110-115°F)
⅓ cup + 2 tablespoons whole or lowfat milk
¼ cup sugar
1 teaspoon salt
¼ cup butter, softened
1 egg
3 cups all-purpose flour

Dissolve the yeast in the water in a small bowl until smooth. Place the milk, sugar, salt and butter in the bowl and blend on ① for a few seconds. Add the yeast and water mixture, along with the egg and blend on ① until smooth. Add 1 cup of flour and blend on ① until well-combined. Clean the sides of the bowl with a plastic spatula and add 1 cup of flour. Blend again on ① until smooth. Clean the sides of the bowl and add the remaining cup of flour. Pulse on ① for about 1 minute, adding flour if needed until the dough holds it's shape into a ball.

Lightly coat a large mixing bowl with cooking spray and place the dough in the bowl. Turn the dough, cover tightly with plastic wrap and refrigerate for 12 hours. Remove and form small balls of dough (about the size of golf balls). Place the balls in a 9-inch by 13-inch baking pan that has been coated with cooking spray. Cover and let rise in a warm place until doubled, about 45 minutes. Bake at 400°F for about 20 minutes, or until golden brown.

YOU'LL NEED:

✓ 40 ounce Bowl
✓ Dough Blade
✓ Bowl Lid

BANANA NUT BREAD

MAKES 1 LOAF

A classic bread for the holidays or any day you want a welcome treat with your hot coffee or tea. Some cooks prefer to cool this bread completely and cut into thin slices before serving with butter or cream cheese.

3 small very ripe bananas, peeled
1 tablespoon lemon juice
½ cup butter
¾ cup sugar
2 eggs
½ cup milk (as needed)
2 cups all-purpose flour
1½ teaspoons baking powder
½ teaspoon salt
½ teaspoon baking soda
¼ cup walnuts

Place the bananas in the bowl and pulse on ① until smooth. Add the lemon juice, butter, sugar, eggs and almost all of the milk. Blend on ① until smooth. Add 1 cup of the flour, baking powder, salt and soda and blend on ① for about 10 seconds. Clean the sides of the bowl and add more milk if needed. Add the walnuts and pulse again briefly.

Lightly coat a 9-inch by 5-inch loaf baking pan with cooking spray. Spoon the batter into the loaf pan and use a knife to evenly spread across the pan. Bake at 350°F for 1 hour, or until the loaf is cooked through and golden brown. Cool on a wire rack.

YOU'LL NEED:

✓ 40 ounce Bowl
✓ Dough Blade
✓ Bowl Lid

PECAN CINNAMON ROLLS

MAKES ABOUT 8-9 ROLLS

These short-cut "one-rise" rolls are perfect for Saturday morning cooks who want to prepare and bake rolls quickly. The aroma of fresh baked rolls will delight the entire household.

¼ oz. pkg. dry active yeast
¼ cup water, warmed to 110-115°F
⅔ cup buttermilk
1 large egg
¼ cup butter, melted
¼ cup sugar
2¾ cups all-purpose flour
1 teaspoon baking powder
1 teaspoon salt

Buttery Pecan Crumble:
¼ cup butter
1 teaspoon ground cinnamon
¼ cup brown sugar, packed
½ cup pecans

Dissolve the yeast in the water and stir well. Pour into the bowl. Add the buttermilk, egg, butter and sugar and blend on ① until smooth. Clean the sides of the bowl with a spatula and add 1 cup of the flour, the baking powder and salt. Blend on ① for 30 seconds. Add the remaining flour and pulse to blend on ① for about 2 minutes, or until the ingredients are well-incorporated. Place the dough on a floured board. Clean the bowl and dry.

Place the butter, cinnamon, brown sugar and pecans into the bowl and blend on ① until uniformly chopped.

Roll the dough into a 12-inch by 7-inch rectangle and sprinkle the pecan butter mixture over the dough. Roll up the dough, beginning at the wide end. Pinch the long edge of the dough to seal. Cut into 12 slices and place in a lightly oiled 9-inch round baking pan. Let rise until doubled, about 60 to 75 minutes.

Bake at 375°F for 25 minutes. Remove and cool the rolls on a wire rack.

YOU'LL NEED:

✓ 40 ounce Bowl
✓ Dough Blade
✓ Blade Assembly
✓ Bowl Lid

DOUBLE LEMON GLAZED CAKE

MAKES 1 CAKE

Tart and tangy, best served in thin slices with crème fraiche or ice cream.

6 tablespoons butter
¾ cup sugar
2 large eggs
zest of 1 lemon (reserve lemon juice)
½ cup lowfat milk
1½ cups all-purpose flour
¼ teaspoon salt
1 teaspoon baking powder

Lemon Glaze:
½ cup sugar
juice of one lemon

Place the butter, sugar, eggs, lemon and milk in the bowl and blend on ① until very smooth. Use a spatula to clean the sides of the blender if needed. Add the flour, salt and baking powder and blend on ① until the batter is smooth again.

Prepare a 9-inch by 5-inch loaf pan by coating with cooking spray. Pour the batter into the prepared pan and bake at 350°F for 1 hour.

As the lemon cake is baking, prepare the glaze by combining the sugar and juice in a small bowl. As soon as the cake is removed from the oven, pour the glaze over the cake. Place the pan on a wire rack to cool. When cool, remove the loaf and slice or refrigerate until use.

YOU'LL NEED:

✓ **40 ounce Bowl**
✓ **Dough Blade**
✓ **Bowl Lid**

CINNAMON & NUTMEG SPICE DONUTS

MAKES 8 TO 9 DONUTS

Yummy! Dust one of these cake donuts with powdered sugar or eat just as they are, crispy, warm and sweet.

2 eggs
1 teaspoon vanilla extract
½ cup sugar
2 tablespoons butter
½ cup milk
2½ cups all-purpose flour
1½ teaspoons baking powder
½ teaspoon salt
¼ teaspoon ground cinnamon
¼ teaspoon ground nutmeg
oil for frying
powdered sugar for garnish

Place the eggs, extract, sugar, butter and milk in the bowl and blend on ① until smooth. Clean the sides of the bowl with a spatula and add 1 cup of the flour, the baking powder, salt, cinnamon and nutmeg. Blend on ① for 30 seconds. Add the remaining flour and pulse on ① until the dough is smooth and well-incorporated.

Place the dough on a lightly floured board and roll into a ½-inch thickness. Cut with a donut cutter.

Choose a deep pan that will hold 3 inches of oil and heat on medium-high heat until 375°F (or use a deep fryer as directed). When the oil is ready, use a slotted spoon to place 3 to 4 donuts in the oil and fry for about 2 minutes. Turn and continue frying for 1 minute, or until both sides are crispy and brown and the donuts are cooked through. Repeat with the remaining donuts and donut holes, if desired. Dust with powdered sugar, if desired.

YOU'LL NEED:

✓ **40 ounce Bowl**
✓ **Dough Blade**
✓ **Bowl Lid**

RULE THE KITCHE

FRESH BLUEBERRY LEMON SCONES

MAKES 16

Scones aren't meant to be light and flaky; they are considered to be a cross between a muffin and bread, so this makes scones perfect for brunch or teatime. Fresh blueberries add antioxidant power to your scones.

¾ cup butter
1 cup buttermilk
1 teaspoon lemon extract
½ cup sugar
3 cups all-purpose flour
2½ teaspoons baking powder
½ teaspoon baking soda
1 cup fresh blueberries, rinsed
sugar for dusting

Preheat the oven to 425°F. Place the butter, buttermilk, extract and sugar in the bowl and blend on ① until very smooth. Add 1 cup of the flour, the baking powder and baking soda and blend again on ① until smooth. Use a spatula to clean the sides of the pitcher as needed. Add 1 cup of flour and blend on ① for about 10 seconds. Add the remaining flour and pulse on ① for about 10 seconds, or until the dough is uniform. Remove the dough blade and lightly fold in the blueberries.

Divide the dough in half on a lightly floured board and pat each half into an 8-inch circle about ½-inch thick. Sprinkle each circle with sugar. Lightly press the sugar into the dough. Cut each round into 8 wedges using a sharp knife. Place the scones on a baking sheet about ½-inch apart and bake for 15 to 18 minutes. Serve while warm.

YOU'LL NEED:

✓ **40 ounce Bowl**
✓ **Dough Blade**
✓ **Bowl Lid**

FRESH PEACH CRISP WITH GINGER WHIPPED CREAM

SERVES 6

The perfectly easy dessert for entertaining guests!

6 peaches, pitted, peeled and roughly chopped
½ cup sugar
2 tablespoons all-purpose flour
½ teaspoon vanilla extract
pinch ground cinnamon
2 tablespoons butter

Crisp Topping:
1 cup all-purpose flour
3 tablespoons sugar
¼ teaspoon ground nutmeg
½ cup almonds, shelled
6 tablespoons butter

Ginger Whipped Cream:
2 cups whipping cream
½ teaspoon fresh ginger, grated
2 tablespoons sugar

Place the peaches in the pitcher and add the sugar. Pulse on ① until the peaches are mashed. Add the flour, extract, cinnamon and butter and pulse on ① for 10 seconds. The batter should be slightly uneven throughout.

Lightly coat a 9-inch x 13-inch baking pan with cooking spray and pour the peach batter into the pan. Clean and dry the pitcher. Place the 1 cup flour, sugar, nutmeg, almonds and butter into the pitcher and blend on ① until finely mixed. Scatter the crisp topping mixture over the peach batter. Clean and dry the pitcher.

Bake at 350°F for 25 minutes until the filling is bubbly. Place the cream in the pitcher and blend on ③ about 35 seconds. Lightly fold in the ginger and sugar. To serve, spoon the peach crisp into bowls and top with each with a large dollop of the whipped cream. Serve at once.

YOU'LL NEED:

✓ **72 ounce Pitcher**
✓ **Blade Assembly**
✓ **Pitcher Lid**

RULE THE KITCHEN

BLUEBERRY MUFFINS

MAKES ABOUT 12 MUFFINS

Super easy and super delicious! Serve while warm with sweet butter.

¾ cup whole milk
1 large egg
½ cup vegetable shortening
2 tablespoons sugar
¾ teaspoon salt
2½ teaspoons baking powder
2 cups all-purpose flour
1 cup fresh blueberries

Place the milk, egg, shortening and sugar in the pitcher and blend on ❶ until smooth. Add the salt, baking powder, and flour and blend on ❶ just until the ingredients are combined. Do not over-process. Remove the batter and fold in the blueberries.

Prepare a 12-cup muffin tin by coating each cup with cooking spray or lining each cup with foil or paper cups. Spoon the batter evenly into the muffin cups. Bake at 400°F for about 25 minutes, or until golden brown.

YOU'LL NEED:

✓ **40 ounce Bowl**
✓ **Dough Blade**
✓ **Bowl Lid**

CHOCOLATE CHUNK MUFFINS

MAKES 12 MUFFINS

Rich, dark and moist, these muffins could almost be labeled "brownies" instead. You decide!

2 cups semi-sweet chocolate chips
¼ cup butter
4 large eggs
¾ cup sugar
1 teaspoon vanilla extract
½ teaspoon salt
1 cup all-purpose flour
1 cup dark chocolate chips
½ cup walnuts
½ cup semi-sweet chocolate chips

Place the 2 cups chocolate chips and the butter in a medium microwave-safe bowl and heat for 1 minute. Stir and microwave again for 1 minute. Stir and repeat until the chips are melted and the mixture is smooth. Spoon the chocolate and butter into the bowl.

Add the eggs, sugar, vanilla, salt and flour. Blend on ① until smooth, cleaning the sides of the bowl with a spatula, if needed. Remove the batter from the blender and add the dark chocolate chips to the batter. Stir to mix well.

Spoon the muffin batter into muffin cups that have been prepared with cupcake or foil liners.

Place the walnuts and remaining chocolate chips into the bowl. Blend on ① until uniformly chopped. Sprinkle the chopped nut and chocolate mixture over the top of each muffin.

Bake at 350°F for 30 to 40 minutes, or until baked through. Cool on a wire rack.

YOU'LL NEED:

✓ **40 ounce Bowl**
✓ **Dough Blade**
✓ **Bowl Lid**

CRANBERRY, ORANGE & WALNUT BREAD

SERVES 8

A welcoming bread at breakfast or snack time. Best when served at room temperature with a schmear of cream cheese or butter.

1 fresh orange, peeled, sectioned, seeds removed

⅓ - ½ cup milk

¼ cup butter

1 cup sugar

1 large egg

2 cups flour

½ teaspoon baking soda

½ teaspoon baking powder

½ teaspoon salt

½ cup dried cranberries

½ cup walnuts, chopped

Place the orange sections in the bowl and blend on ① until fairly smooth. Strain the juice and discard the solids. Add enough milk to the juice to equal ¾ cup. Place the juice/milk mixture in the bowl and add the butter, sugar and egg. Blend on ① for 10 seconds.

Add 1 cup of the flour, the baking soda and powder and salt and blend on ① until smooth. Clean the sides of the bowl with a spatula and add the remaining flour, blending on ① until just combined. Remove the dough blade and fold in the cranberries and walnuts.

Lightly coat a 9-inch by 5-inch loaf pan with cooking spray and spoon the batter into the pan. Bake at 350°F for 50-60 minutes, or until the bread is baked throughout.

YOU'LL NEED:

✓ 40 ounce Bowl
✓ Dough Blade
✓ Bowl Lid

RULE THE KITCHE

CHICKEN
FETTUCINI
ALFREDO
P. 133

CHAPTER SEVEN

Entrées, Salads
& Sides

SAUSAGE AND ROASTED VEGETABLE PENNE PASTA

MAKES 4 TO 6 SERVINGS

Fennel has a mild anise flavor and adds a sweet, warm earthy flavor to the roasted vegetable sauce. A delicious way to get a garden-full of vegetables on everyone's plate!

4 zucchini, halved lengthwise and cut into 1 inch pieces
2 medium onions, peeled and quartered
6 large cloves garlic, peeled
6 ripe Roma tomatoes, cored and quartered lengthwise
1 bulb fennel, trimmed and cut into 1 inch pieces
¼ cup + 1 tablespoon extra-virgin olive oil
1 teaspoon salt
1 teaspoon freshly ground black pepper
4 large pre-cooked chicken pesto sausages, sliced into 1 inch pieces
16 ounce pkg penne pasta, uncooked
1 cup chicken stock
½ cup white wine
2 tablespoons fresh basil leaves, chopped
1 tablespoon fresh oregano, chopped
½ cup Parmesan cheese, freshly grated

YOU'LL NEED:

✓ 72 ounce Pitcher
✓ Blade Assembly
✓ Pitcher Lid

Preheat the oven to 400°F degrees. Place the zucchini, onions, garlic, tomatoes, and fennel in a large mixing bowl and toss with ¼ cup olive oil, salt and pepper. Arrange the vegetables loosely on 2 baking sheets lined with parchment paper; do not crowd. Roast vegetables for 15 to 20 minutes. Vegetables will be soft and slightly browned when done.

While the vegetables are roasting, brown the pre-cooked sausage in a large skillet in 1 tablespoon of olive oil. Prepare the penne pasta according to package directions. When the pasta is done, drain in a colander, retaining a few cups of pasta water. Keep the pasta warm by placing the colander over a bowl of the retained warm pasta water.

Place half of each type of roasted vegetable, in batches, into the pitcher. Pulse on ❶ into a rough sauce, transferring each processed batch to the empty pasta stockpot. To the last batch, add chicken stock, wine, basil and oregano and process on ❶ until blended. Add to the vegetables in stockpot, set heat to medium-low and stir in the remaining un-blended roasted vegetables and chicken sausage. Thin the sauce, if desired, with additional chicken stock or water. Place the pasta in large serving bowl, add the sauce and toss. Garnish with the Parmesan cheese.

NEW MEXICAN RED CHILE CHEESE ENCHILADAS

SERVES 4

Your family will request these scrumptious enchiladas again and again. Homemade is always so much better! New Mexican red chile pods are available in cello bags at your local grocery store in the Ethnic Food aisle.

14 dried New Mexican red chile pods
3 cups water
6 cloves garlic, peeled
½ teaspoon ground cumin, or more to taste
½ teaspoon Mexican oregano
½ teaspoon salt
1 large white onion, peeled and diced
4 ounce can chopped black olives
2 tablespoons canola oil, divided
8 corn tortillas
3 cups Jack cheese, shredded
½ head iceberg lettuce, thinly shredded
2 ripe tomatoes, cored and chopped
1 avocado, peeled, pitted and diced
4 dollops sour cream

Preheat the oven to 350°F degrees. Remove the stems and seeds of the chile pods and place the pods in a medium saucepan. Add water to the pan and simmer over low heat for about 10 minutes. Transfer the chiles and soaking water to the pitcher, add the garlic and blend on ③ until smooth.

Return the pureed chile sauce to the sauce pan, adding the cumin, Mexican oregano, and salt. Bring just to a boil, reduce the heat and simmer for 10 minutes, stirring occasionally. In a small bowl, mix the chopped onion with the black olives and set aside.

Heat 1 teaspoon canola oil in a 10-inch skillet over medium heat. Quickly fry the tortillas, one at a time, for about 5 to 10 seconds per side, just to soften and add flavor. Do not fry to the crispy stage. Add more oil to the pan between batches as necessary, reheating as you go. Transfer the tortillas to paper towels to drain. ▸

YOU'LL NEED:

✓ 72 ounce Pitcher
✓ Blade Assembly
✓ Pitcher Lid

RULE THE KITCHE

Dip a softened tortilla in the red chile sauce to coat and place the tortilla on a plate. Place 2 tablespoons of cheese and one-eighth of the onion-olive mixture down the center of the tortilla. Roll the tortilla and place in a baking dish, seam side down. Repeat with the remaining tortillas. Pour the remaining sauce over the rolled tortillas and sprinkle the remaining cheese over the top.

Bake uncovered for about 20 minutes until the cheese is melted and turning golden brown. When done, the enchiladas will be piping hot throughout. Serve 2 enchiladas per person garnished with shredded lettuce, chopped tomato, avocado and a dollop of sour cream.

CHICKEN FETTUCCINI ALFREDO

MAKES 4 SERVINGS

Your guests will never know how simple it was to create this stylish and sumptuous dish. A simple green salad and crusty French bread complete the scene.

2 tablespoons extra-virgin olive oil
2 skinless, boneless chicken breast halves, cut into
1 inch pieces
½ teaspoon salt
1 teaspoon freshly ground black pepper
16 ounce pkg. fettuccini noodles, uncooked
½ cup unsalted butter
2 cups heavy cream
1½ cups + ½ cup Parmesan cheese, freshly grated
1 teaspoon freshly ground black pepper
4 tablespoons fresh flat-leaf Italian parsley, chopped

In a large skillet, heat the oil over medium-high heat. Add the chicken, sprinkle with salt and pepper and sauté, stirring frequently, until lightly browned on all sides and cooked through. Do not crowd the pan, cook in batches if necessary.

Prepare the fettuccini according to package directions. When the pasta is done, drain in a colander, retaining a few cups of pasta water. Keep the pasta warm by placing a colander over a bowl of the retained pasta water.

Melt the butter in small sauce pan over low heat or in a microwave. Pour the heavy cream, melted butter and 1½ cups grated cheese into the pitcher and blend on ① until smooth. Do not over mix. Transfer to a large sauté pan over low heat and cook, stirring frequently. When the sauce is hot and thickening, add the cooked fettuccini and chicken, gently tossing to coat with the sauce. Serve garnished with chopped parsley and the remainder of the Parmesan cheese.

YOU'LL NEED:

✓ 72 ounce Pitcher
✓ Blade Assembly
✓ Pitcher Lid

RULE THE KITCHE

BAKED TOMATILLO CHICKEN

SERVES 4

A memorable dish from a super simple "made from scratch" salsa. The chicken is almost poached in the sauce and is so tender you can cut it with a fork. Make extra and serve the tomatillo "salsa" with chips!

1 pound fresh tomatillos

1 large white onion, peeled and cut into chunks

3 cloves garlic, peeled

1 Serrano chile pepper

½ packed cup cilantro leaves

½ teaspoon salt

1 large lime, juiced (about 2 tablespoons)

4 skinless, boneless chicken breast halves

Remove the husks from the tomatillos and wash under running water until the tomatillos are no longer sticky. Cut each into quarters. Place into the pitcher and add the onion, garlic and Serrano pepper and pulse on **1** until roughly chopped. Add the cilantro, salt and lime juice and continue blending until the mixture is well-combined.

Preheat the oven to 350°F degrees. Place the chicken breasts in a baking dish and cover with the tomatillo sauce. Cover with foil and bake for 20 minutes. Remove the foil and continue baking for 5 to 10 minutes longer or until the chicken is cooked through and no pink remains.

YOU'LL NEED:

✓ 72 ounce Pitcher

✓ Blade Assembly

✓ Pitcher Lid

PORK CHOPS
WITH PROVENCE PRUNE SAUCE

SERVES 2

Browning and baking in the same pan saves time and clean-up! This luscious sauce cooks into the pork giving it and elegant flavor. Spoon the sauce over the pork chops and add baked fingerling potatoes.

10 prunes, pitted and roughly chopped
½ cup brandy
½ cup chicken stock
2 teaspoons dried sage
3 pieces apple smoked bacon, chopped
2 shallots, peeled and finely chopped
2 boneless pork chops, each 1½ inch thick
1 tablespoon extra-virgin olive oil
½ teaspoon freshly ground black pepper

Place prunes and brandy in a small saucepan over medium heat and cook until small bubbles begin to form at the sides, reduce the heat to low and simmer for 20 minutes, until the prunes are softened. Place half of the prune/brandy mixture into the pitcher and add the chicken stock and sage. Blend on ❷ until the mixture is smooth.

Preheat the oven to 350°F degrees. In an oven-proof skillet, sauté the bacon and shallots over medium-high heat until the shallots begin to caramelize and the bacon is crispy. Using a slotted spoon, remove the bacon/shallot mixture, leaving some of the drippings, and set aside.

Pat the pork chops dry and lightly rub both sides with olive oil and sprinkle with pepper. Return the skillet to medium-high heat; add the pork chops when the pan is hot and brown on both sides. Reduce the heat to medium, return the shallots and bacon to pan, add the pureed prune sauce and remaining chopped prunes with the brandy. Place the skillet in the oven, cover with foil and bake for 30 to 40 minutes, or until the chops are 150°F internally. Allow the meat to rest for a few minutes before serving. Spoon any remaining sauce over the chops and serve.

YOU'LL NEED:

✓ 72 ounce Pitcher
✓ Blade Assembly
✓ Pitcher Lid

RULE THE KITCHE

ITALIAN-STUFFED PORK TENDERLOIN

MAKES 6 TO 8 SERVINGS

Tantalize your guests with the scrumptious flavors of apricots, cognac and thyme.

1 cup cognac or brandy
¾ cup dried apricots, roughly chopped
2 thick slices stale or day old hearty French bread, crusts removed
2 small shallots, peeled
2 cloves garlic, peeled
3 fresh thyme leaves, torn
2 tablespoons unsalted butter
2 teaspoons extra-virgin olive oil, divided
2 pork tenderloins, each ¾ to 1 pound
1 teaspoon freshly ground black pepper
4 ounces thinly sliced Prosciutto (about 8 slices)
½ teaspoon salt

Preheat the oven to 375°F degrees. Heat the brandy in a small sauce pan over low heat. Cool slightly, add the dried apricots and soak until soft and plump. Drain the fruit and let cool, reserving 1 tablespoon of the soaking brandy.

Tear the French bread into large pieces, place into the pitcher and pulse on ❶ until the bread is completely crumbled. Set aside. Place the shallots, garlic and thyme leaves in the blender and pulse on ❶ until finely chopped.

In a large oven-proof skillet, heat the butter and 1 teaspoon olive oil over medium high heat. Add the shallot and garlic mixture and sauté, stirring often, for about 3 minutes. Stir in the apricots and reserved brandy, cooking until the brandy has evaporated. Stir in the bread crumbs, mixing well.

Butterfly each pork loin and pound between plastic wrap to an even thickness. Sprinkle ½ teaspoon

YOU'LL NEED:

✓ **72 ounce Pitcher**
✓ **Blade Assembly**
✓ **Pitcher Lid**

pepper on the inside of the butterflied pork and cover with prosciutto slices. Spread the apricot-bread crumb mixture over the prosciutto, leaving about a ½ inch border around the edges. Starting on a long side, pull the meat up and over the filling, and roll into a thick log. Tie with butcher's twine to seal. Salt and pepper the outside of the pork loins.

Heat the remaining teaspoon of olive oil in the skillet over medium high heat. Place the pork tenderloins in the pan and sear, turning to brown on all sides. Transfer the skillet to the preheated oven and roast, uncovered for 35 to 40 minutes, until an inserted meat thermometer registers 160°F degrees, for medium done. When done, allow the pork tenderloin to rest for a couple of minutes, remove the twine, slice diagonally and serve.

TIP

It's always wise to remove the meat a bit earlier than called for because the meat will continue cooking as it stands for a few minutes.

MINI CRAB RAMEKINS

SERVES 4

With all the flavors of Maryland crab cakes, this is easy to do ahead. Serve with a salad of field greens and mild, sweet dinner rolls.

8 slices stale or day old white bread, crusts removed
¼ cup unsalted butter
1 cup regular or lowfat mayonnaise
2 teaspoons Dijon mustard
1½ teaspoons Worcestershire sauce
2 eggs, lightly beaten
2 teaspoons Chesapeake Bay Style seafood seasoning
2 6 ounce cans lump crabmeat, drained (or 12 to 16 ounces fresh crabmeat)
2 medium shallots, minced
2 medium inside ribs of celery, with leaves, washed, tough strings removed, minced

1 teaspoon fresh lemon juice
1 tablespoon fresh parsley, chopped
1 teaspoon freshly ground black pepper

Preheat the oven to 350°F degrees. Cut the bread into large pieces, place into the pitcher and pulse on ❶ until the bread is completely crumbled. Melt the butter in a small saucepan over low heat or in a microwave, mix with the bread crumbs and set aside.

Place the mayonnaise, mustard, Worcestershire sauce, eggs, and seafood seasoning in the pitcher and blend on ❷ until well-combined. Pick through crabmeat and remove any cartilage or shell fragments and add to the mixture along with all remaining ingredients, reserving ½ of the buttered bread crumbs. Pulse on ❶ to combine. Divide the mixture among buttered individual ramekins and top with the remaining buttered bread crumbs.

Bake for 25 to 30 minutes until the tops are golden brown and the crab casseroles are piping hot. Serve warm with garnishes of lemon juice, parsley and black pepper. Add a crusty French bread to round out this entrée.

YOU'LL NEED:

✓ 72 ounce Pitcher
✓ Blade Assembly
✓ Pitcher Lid

SMOKED PAPRIKA CHICKEN PASTA IN SWEET RED PEPPER SAUCE

MAKES 6 TO 8 SERVINGS

Smoky sweet paprika defines this luscious entrée.

3 red bell peppers, seeded and coarsely chopped
3 cloves garlic, peeled
1 medium white onion, peeled and quartered
¼ cup toasted pine nuts
2 teaspoons smoked paprika, divided
1½ teaspoon salt, divided
1½ teaspoon freshly ground black pepper, divided
½ cup white flour
2 tablespoons canola oil
4 boneless, skinless, chicken breasts, cubed
1 cup chicken stock
½ cup heavy cream
2 zucchini, halved lengthwise and cut into 1 inch pieces
½ cup parsley, chopped
16 ounce pkg rigatoni pasta, uncooked
½ cup Parmesan cheese, freshly grated

Place the bell peppers, garlic, onion, pine nuts, 1 teaspoon smoked paprika, ½ teaspoon salt and ½ teaspoon black pepper into the pitcher and blend on ① into a rough, but uniform pulp.

Place the flour, 1 teaspoon each of salt, pepper and paprika in self-sealing plastic bag. Add the chicken pieces in batches, shaking to coat with the flour. Heat 2 tablespoons of oil in a large skillet over medium-high heat. When the oil is hot, fry the chicken until golden brown on all sides and cooked through, with no pink remaining. Do not crowd the pan; cook in batches if needed. Remove the fried chicken and keep warm.

Clean the skillet and add the blender sauce, stock, cream, zucchini and parsley. Heat on medium and cook for 10 to 15 minutes, stirring often. Add the chicken and adjust the seasonings, if desired. Prepare the rigatoni according to package directions. When the pasta is done, drain and place in a large shallow serving bowl, add the sauce and toss to mix well. Garnish the pasta with freshly grated Parmesan cheese.

YOU'LL NEED:

✓ **72 ounce Pitcher**
✓ **Blade Assembly**
✓ **Pitcher Lid**

139

SPAGHETTI MARINARA

MAKES 3 CUPS SAUCE – ENOUGH FOR 4 TO 6 SERVINGS

Fresh and simple flavors create a fast classic that is as healthy as it is flavorful. The olive oil adds richness but may be omitted with good results for a lower fat version of this sauce. Use as a pasta sauce, or to create dishes such as chicken parmesan or baked lasagna. Freezes well for up to 2 months.

28 ounce can whole peeled tomatoes, with juice from can
¼ cup tightly packed fresh basil leaves
½ medium yellow onion, peeled and quartered
3 cloves garlic, peeled
½ cup water
½ cup good red wine
½ teaspoon salt
½ teaspoon freshly ground black pepper
1 tablespoon extra-virgin olive oil
16 ounce pkg spaghetti noodles, uncooked
½ cup Parmesan cheese, freshly grated

Place all of the ingredients except the olive oil, spaghetti noodles and Parmesan cheese into the pitcher and blend on ❷ until the vegetables are finely chopped and the sauce is semi-smooth. In a large skillet, heat the oil over medium heat. Add the sauce from the blender, stir to incorporate the oil, reduce the heat to low and simmer the sauce, partially covered, for 15 minutes.

Prepare the spaghetti according to package directions. When the pasta is done, drain in a colander, and transfer the cooked pasta to a large serving bowl. Pour the sauce over the pasta and toss gently to coat. Top with the Parmesan cheese just before serving.

YOU'LL NEED:

✓ 72 ounce Pitcher
✓ Blade Assembly
✓ Pitcher Lid

CREAMY SCALLOPED POTATOES

MAKES 4 TO 6 SERVINGS

The *Ninja™Blender* takes the work out of making a smooth cream sauce. Add your favorite cheese and butter to make this quick cheese sauce that spreads over tender potatoes. Yum!

1 cup whole milk
1 cup heavy cream
1 tablespoon fresh thyme leaves
½ teaspoon ground nutmeg
4 tablespoons white flour
4 tablespoons softened butter
2 pounds russet potatoes, peeled and cut into
1/8-inch thick slices
pinch salt
pinch freshly ground black pepper
1 cup Parmesan cheese, grated

Preheat the oven to 375°F degrees. Place the milk, cream, thyme, nutmeg and flour into the pitcher and blend on ❷ until smooth. Transfer to a saucepan, and cook on medium heat, stirring constantly until the mixture is slightly thickened, about 5 minutes. Butter a 9-inch by 11-inch baking dish. Place a layer of potato slices in the pan in an overlapping pattern and sprinkle with salt and pepper. Remove the sauce from the heat and pour one-third of the sauce over the potatoes. Top with ¼ cup Parmesan cheese.

Repeat this process, creating 2 layers, ending with a final dusting of Parmesan cheese. Add more cheese to top, if desired. Bake, uncovered, for 45 minutes until the top is golden brown and slightly crunchy and the potatoes are cooked through and semi-blended with the sauce.

YOU'LL NEED:

✓ 72 ounce Pitcher
✓ Blade Assembly
✓ Pitcher Lid

MIDDLE EASTERN TABOULI

SERVES 6

A traditional Middle Eastern dish made with bulgur wheat, which is found in the bulk food or Ethnic Food section at your local grocery store. A great dish to make when you have extra tomatoes or lemons that need to be used.

1 cup plain bulgur (cracked wheat), uncooked
1 cup water
1 bunch fresh parsley, stemmed
6 sprigs fresh mint, stemmed
½ small white onion, peeled
2 cloves garlic, peeled
⅓ cup extra virgin olive oil
2 lemons, juiced (about ¼ cup)
½ teaspoon salt
½ teaspoon freshly ground black pepper
2 ripe tomatoes, cored and diced
3 green onions, cleaned and chopped

In a large bowl, mix the bulgur with the water. Cover and let stand for 20 minutes, until the water is absorbed and the wheat is tender.

Place the parsley, mint, onion and garlic into the bowl and pulse on ❶ to make a small, rough chop, cleaning the sides of the bowl with a spatula as necessary. Transfer the mixture to the bowl of softened bulgur.

Place the olive oil, lemon juice, salt and pepper in the bowl and blend on ❶ until incorporated. Add the dressing to the bulgur mixture and lightly toss to mix. Add the chopped tomatoes and green onion, again tossing gently to mix. Taste and adjust the seasonings. Serve well-chilled or at room temperature.

YOU'LL NEED:

✓ 40 ounce Bowl
✓ Blade Assembly
✓ Bowl Lid

RULE THE KITCHE

CAESAR SALAD WITH GARLIC CROUTONS

SERVES 4

This universal classic was invented by Italian restaurateur Caesar Cardini at his famous restaurant in Tijuana in the 1920s. His famous dressing is available at the grocery store, but the *Ninja™ Blender* makes it so easy – you might as well make your own! Please note that there are raw eggs in this dressing.

Caesar Salad Dressing
2 large egg yolks
2 teaspoons Worcestershire sauce
3 large lemons, juiced (6 tablespoons)
2 cloves garlic, peeled
½ teaspoon salt
1 teaspoon freshly ground black pepper
8 anchovy fillets or 3 teaspoons anchovy paste
2 teaspoons Dijon mustard
⅔ cup extra-virgin olive oil
⅔ cup Parmesan cheese, grated

For croutons and salad:
2 large cloves garlic, peeled and minced
¼ cup extra-virgin olive oil

1 small French baguette, cut into 1 inch cups
4 hearts romaine lettuce, torn into small pieces
Freshly shaved parmesan cheese, for topping

Place the egg yolks, Worcestershire sauce, lemon juice, 2 cloves garlic, salt, pepper, anchovy fillets or paste and mustard into the pitcher and blend on ❷ until the mixture is very smooth. With the blender running, slowly pour two-thirds cup olive oil through the top pouring tab in a steady stream to emulsify the dressing. Add the Parmesan cheese and pulse on ❶ to blend. Cover and refrigerate until ready to use.

Preheat the oven to 350°F degrees. Combine 2 cloves of the minced garlic, ¼ cup oil, and bread cups in a bowl and toss to coat. Spread the bread cups onto a baking sheet and bake, watching carefully, until golden brown, about 10 minutes.

To assemble the salads, place the torn lettuce in a large bowl, toss with the dressing and top with the croutons and shaved Parmesan cheese. Serve at once.

YOU'LL NEED:

✓ 72 ounce Pitcher
✓ Blade Assembly
✓ Pitcher Lid

TANGY SUMMER FRUIT SALAD

MAKES 4 TO 6 SERVINGS

Sweetened fruit topped with a dollop of tart yogurt is the perfect refresher on a hot summer day.

1 cup tightly packed fresh mint leaves
⅓ cup superfine sugar
1 pound fresh strawberries, cleaned, hulled and halved
1 pound fresh blackberries, cleaned and dried
3 firm-ripe peaches or nectarines, pitted, and cut into chunks
1 medium honeydew melon, halved, seeded and cut into bite-sized chunks
1 cup Greek yogurt

Place the mint leaves and sugar into the pitcher and blend on ① until finely ground. Mix the fruit in a large serving bowl and toss with the desired amount of minted sugar. Serve in individual bowls topped with a dollop of Greek yogurt.

TIP

What's the difference between typical plain yogurt and Greek yogurt? Greek yogurt is thicker and more rich-tasting than plain yogurt. It is often higher in protein and lower in sugar than plain yogurt.

YOU'LL NEED:

✓ 72 ounce Pitcher
✓ Blade Assembly
✓ Pitcher Lid

BLT SALAD
WITH BLUE CHEESE DRESSING

MAKES ABOUT 2 CUPS DRESSING; ENOUGH SALAD FOR 4

This classic salad is like a BLT without the bread! A firm and heavy head of iceberg makes a superior salad. It's worth taking the time in the market to find just the right one.

4 ounces good quality Blue cheese
½ cup regular mayonnaise
½ cup sour cream
½ cup buttermilk
1 tablespoon tarragon vinegar
½ teaspoon salt
½ teaspoon freshly ground black pepper
1 firm head iceberg lettuce, cut into 4 large wedges
1 ripe tomato, sliced
1 cup fresh bacon crumbles

Place the Blue cheese, mayonnaise, sour cream, buttermilk, vinegar, salt and pepper into the bowl and blend on ① until smooth.

Place a wedge of iceberg lettuce on each serving plate. Pour one-fourth of the dressing on each of the lettuce wedges, place tomato slices on the side and top with bacon crumbles.

YOU'LL NEED:

✓ **40 ounce Bowl**
✓ **Blade Assembly**
✓ **Bowl Lid**

BALSAMIC & STRAWBERRY VINAIGRETTE

MAKES ABOUT 1¼ CUPS

A rich and sweet vinaigrette that dresses up any salad. Try tossing dried cranberries, toasted pecans and apples with field greens to give this dressing a boost!

¼ cup fresh strawberries, hulled and chopped
1 tablespoon strawberry jam
¼ teaspoon salt
⅛ teaspoon freshly ground black pepper
2 tablespoons balsamic vinegar
¾ cup extra virgin olive oil

Place the strawberries, jam, salt, pepper and vinegar into the bowl and blend on until very smooth. With the blender running, slowly pour the olive oil through the top pour tab in a steady stream to emulsify the dressing. Taste and adjust the flavors.

✳ TIP

This dressing quickly becomes a sumptuous summer sauce when heated slightly and brushed over fish or chicken while grilling.

YOU'LL NEED:

√ 40 ounce Bowl
√ Blade Assembly
√ Bowl Lid

APPLE, CRANBERRY & GORGONZOLA SALAD

SERVES 4

Refreshing and appealing! Perfect when serving fish or chicken as your entrée.

2 large Fuji apples, cored and roughly chopped
1 medium cucumber, peeled and roughly cut
½ cup walnuts, halved
1 cup dried cranberries
½ cup gorgonzola cheese, crumbled
½ cup sour cream
¼ cup cream cheese
2 tablespoons milk
pinch salt
pinch black pepper
1 large cucumber, thinly sliced horizontally

Place the apples in the pitcher and blend on **1** until chopped. Remove the apples and place in a mixing bowl. Place the cucumber and walnuts in the pitcher. Blend on **1** for a few seconds until roughly chopped. Remove and add to the apples. Add the dried cranberries and toss. Set aside.

Place the cheese, sour cream, cream cheese, milk, salt and pepper in the pitcher. Blend on **1** until mostly smooth. Remove and set aside.

To serve, form the long slices of cucumber into circular shapes and use a wooden pick to secure. Place each on a salad plate. Fill the cucumber cups with the apple, cucumber mixture and top each salad with the gorgonzola salad dressing.

YOU'LL NEED:

✓ 72 ounce Pitcher
✓ Blade Assembly
✓ Pitcher Lid

KANSAS CITY
BARBECUE SAUCE
P. 156

CHAPTER EIGHT
Marinades, Rubs
& Mopping Sauces

TERIYAKI GRILLING MARINADE

MAKES ABOUT 2 CUPS

After removing the meat from this marinade, pour the marinade into a saucepan, bring to a boil, and simmer for 5 minutes, making a luscious sauce for your grilled masterpiece.

2 cloves garlic, peeled

2 tablespoons fresh ginger, peeled and roughly chopped

¼ white onion, peeled

¼ cup fresh cilantro, stemmed

¾ cup soy sauce

½ cup rice wine vinegar

2 teaspoons Asian chile paste

1 tablespoon honey

2 tablespoons fresh lime juice

¾ teaspoon toasted sesame oil

Place the garlic, ginger, onion and cilantro into the pitcher and pulse on ❷ until uniformly chopped. Add the remaining ingredients and blend on ❷ until mixed well, but with a slightly chunky consistency. Add a little chicken stock or water to thin, if desired.

✳ TIP

Pour this marinade into a self-sealing plastic bag and add a 1½ pound beef flank steak. Seal and marinate for 24 hours. Remove the steak, pat dry and grill for about 8 minutes per side over medium-high heat. Let rest for 5 minutes, then slice thinly across the grain. The result? Perfectly tender and flavorful teriyaki steak!

YOU'LL NEED:

✓ 72 ounce Pitcher

✓ Blade Assembly

✓ Pitcher Lid

SMOKING CHIPOTLE SAUCE

MAKES ABOUT 1 CUP

A chipotle is a dried, smoked jalapeño pepper with a spicy, smoky, slightly sweet flavor. It is often canned in a vinegary sauce called adobo. Add chipotles to stews, soups, sauces and salsas. Use it sparingly until you determine how much "fire" you want to add to your favorite foods!

3 chipotles, canned in adobo sauce, or less if a milder sauce is desired
1 tablespoon adobo sauce from canned chipotles
4 cloves garlic, peeled
2 oranges, peeled and pulled into quarters
1 lime, juiced
1 tablespoon tomato paste
2 tablespoons apple cider vinegar
1 tablespoon extra virgin olive oil
1 teaspoon ground cumin (or more to taste)
1 teaspoon Mexican oregano
½ teaspoon salt
½ teaspoon freshly ground black pepper

Place all ingredients into the pitcher and blend on ❷ until smooth. Transfer to a medium sauce pan, over medium heat and bring to a boil. Reduce the heat to medium-low and simmer, stirring frequently, for 5 to 10 minutes. Thin with a little water if necessary. Cover and store in the refrigerator until use.

✳ TIP

All of the citrus acid in this recipe – oranges, lime, and apple cider vinegar – combine to tenderize meat perfectly. You can use this sauce alongside your favorite grilled meat, or pour the sauce into a self-sealing plastic bag with beef, chicken or pork before grilling and marinate it for a few hours.

YOU'LL NEED:

✓ 72 ounce Pitcher
✓ Blade Assembly
✓ Pitcher Lid

LEMON & HERB MARINADE

MAKES ABOUT 1 CUP

This marinade also works beautifully as a tangy fresh salad dressing.

2 lemons, juiced (4 to 6 tablespoons)
¾ cup extra-virgin olive oil
1 tablespoon fresh thyme leaves
1 small sprig fresh parsley
1 small piece fresh oregano
½ teaspoon salt
½ teaspoon freshly ground black pepper

Place all ingredients into the pitcher and blend on ❷ until smooth. Taste and adjust the flavors to your liking. Use right away or cover and store in the refrigerator. If chilled, let stand at room temperature for 10 minutes to allow the oil to liquefy before serving.

TIP

Makes a light marinade for white fish fillets. Marinate the fish in the refrigerator for no more than one hour. Broil or grill and serve with lemon slices.

YOU'LL NEED:

✓ 72 ounce Pitcher
✓ Blade Assembly
✓ Pitcher Lid

ORANGE PAPAYA SHRIMP MARINADE

SERVES 4 TO 6

A fruity marinade with a spicy Asian twist. Serve fabulous char-grilled shrimp over a bed of aromatic jasmine rice.

1 medium papaya, peeled and quartered
1 medium orange, peeled and pulled into quarters
2 limes, juiced
2 green onions, cleaned, root end removed
2 tablespoons fresh basil leaves
¾ cup soy sauce
1 cup water
2 tablespoons honey
½ teaspoon Five Spice Powder (or more to taste)
2 pounds fresh shrimp, deveined and cleaned, tails removed

Pulse the papaya and orange in the pitcher on ❶ until roughly chopped. Add the remaining ingredients, except the shrimp, and blend on ❸ until the marinade is well combined and semi-smooth. Taste and adjust the flavors and consistency, if desired. Pour the marinade over the shrimp in a self-sealing plastic bag. Seal and refrigerate for at least 30 minutes or longer for a more intense flavor. Discard the marinade and place the shrimp on skewers. Grill the shrimp skewers for about 3 minutes per side. Makes about 1½ cups marinade.

YOU'LL NEED:

✓ 72 ounce Pitcher
✓ Blade Assembly
✓ Pitcher Lid

RULE THE KITC

KANSAS CITY BBQ SAUCE

MAKES ABOUT 3 CUPS

Kansas City, Missouri is considered by many to be the barbeque capitol of America. No wonder with over 100 barbecue restaurants in the city!

1 cup ketchup

¼ cup apple cider vinegar

¼ medium white onion, peeled

2 cloves garlic, peeled

1 cup tomato sauce

¼ cup brown sugar, packed

2 tablespoons molasses

2 tablespoons fresh lemon juice

1½ teaspoons smoked paprika

1 teaspoon freshly ground black pepper

½ teaspoon red chile powder

½ teaspoon salt

Place the ketchup, vinegar, onion and garlic into the pitcher and blend on ❶ until smooth. Add the remaining ingredients and continue blending on ❷ until the sauce is semi-smooth.

Transfer the sauce to a medium saucepan and simmer, stirring occasionally, over low heat for 20 minutes, or until the sauce reduces by one-third. Cover and store in the refrigerator.

✳TIP

For smoking, for grilling, for marinating, for barbeque beans – this sauce does it all!

YOU'LL NEED:

✓ 72 ounce Pitcher

✓ Blade Assembly

✓ Pitcher Lid

SWEET PAPRIKA RUB

MAKES ¾ CUP

A fragrant and flavorful dry rub for a roast chicken or turkey that also creates tasty drippings for gravy.

½ cup firmly packed brown sugar
2 tablespoons sweet paprika
2 teaspoons onion powder
2 teaspoons dry mustard
1 teaspoon crushed red pepper
½ teaspoon salt
½ teaspoon garlic powder
½ teaspoon celery seed

Place all ingredients into the pitcher and pulse on ❶ for 10 seconds, until the spices and sugar are well combined. Use right away or store in an airtight pitcher, in a dark, dry area, for up to 6 months.

✳TIP

Smoked Hungarian sweet paprika is a specialty food item, however you can usually find it in kitchen shops, or in the ethnic food aisle of your grocery store. You can also order it easily online from various outlets. Sweet paprika opens up an entirely new flavor dimension versus the tinned ground paprika we typically use. Once you try sweet paprika, you'll probably never reach for that old tin again.

YOU'LL NEED:

✓ 72 ounce Pitcher
✓ Blade Assembly
✓ Pitcher Lid

RULE THE KITC

GREEK HERB RUB

MAKES 1¾ CUPS

Bring the Mediterranean into your kitchen with this very aromatic rub! It is wonderful on all meats and fish, and especially on roast lamb.

½ cup dried Greek oregano
½ cup dried thyme
¼ cup dried parsley
¼ cup dried marjoram
1 tablespoon dried dill (optional)
1 teaspoon freshly ground black pepper
½ teaspoon salt
¼ cup extra virgin olive oil

Place all ingredients, except the olive oil, into the pitcher and pulse on ❶ for 10 to 20 seconds. Transfer the herbs to a mixing bowl, add oil and toss to just coat the spices. Use right away or store in an airtight pitcher, in a dark, dry area, for up to 6 months.

✳TIP

It's best to let this rub sit for at least 6 to 8 hours before using. This will allow the flavors to marry into each other and the oil will be better absorbed. Slather it over any cut prior to grilling for a fabulous treat.

YOU'LL NEED:

✓ 72 ounce Pitcher
✓ Blade Assembly
✓ Pitcher Lid

CHILI PEPPER HOT SAUCE

MAKES ABOUT 3½

This is the original recipe for what is known as "Tabasco Sauce™." If Tabasco chiles are unavailable, use cayenne or piquins. Dried chiles will also work in a pinch, just let the chiles soak in the simmering sauce until softened.

1 pound fresh red Tabasco chiles, roughly chopped
2 cups white vinegar
2 teaspoons salt

In a medium saucepan, over medium-low heat, combine the chiles, vinegar and salt and simmer for 5 minutes. Remove from the heat and cool. Pour into the pitcher and blend on ❷ until semi-smooth.

Strain the sauce into a glass pitcher with a tight fitting lid and refrigerate for 2 weeks. Strain again before using and if needed, add more vinegar to thin. Return any unused sauce to the pitcher and store in the refrigerator for up to 6 months.

✳TIP

Use with caution! These fiery chiles will melt your tongue and inflame your senses so adjust to the sauce slowly and with great deliberation!

YOU'LL NEED:

✓ 72 ounce Pitcher
✓ Blade Assembly
✓ Pitcher Lid

RULE THE KITC

COWBOY MOPPING SAUCE

MAKES ABOUT 2 CUPS

A thinner sauce than most marinades or barbeque sauces, mopping sauce got its name from the small slathering "mops" used for basting the meat during cooking. The purpose of a mopping sauce is to keep meat moist and add flavor during grilling. Due to the low sugar content it is not prone to burn.

¼ small white onion, peeled

2 cloves fresh garlic, peeled

½ cup white wine vinegar

12 ounce can regular beer, not light

1 lemon, juiced

2 teaspoons Dijon mustard

½ teaspoon freshly ground black pepper

½ teaspoon salt

½ teaspoon ground paprika

½ teaspoon cayenne pepper

Place the onion, garlic and vinegar into the pitcher and blend on ❷, cleaning the pitcher with a spatula as needed, until finely chopped. Add the remaining ingredients and continue processing until smooth. Use right away or cover and store in refrigerator.

✳TIP

Perfect for guys who like the thrill of the grill, this sauce is great for multiple bastings as the meat cooks. Use it liberally!

YOU'LL NEED:

✓ 72 ounce Pitcher

✓ Blade Assembly

✓ Pitcher Lid

THE KITCHEN

BALSAMIC GRILLING SAUCE

MAKES ABOUT 1½ CUPS

This delicious sauce will create a tasty char on grilled meat.

2 tablespoons olive oil
1 large shallot, peeled and minced
1 cup balsamic vinegar
¾ cup ketchup
2 tablespoons brown sugar
1 tablespoon garlic mustard
½ teaspoon salt
½ teaspoon freshly ground black pepper

Heat the oil in a small saucepan over medium heat; add the shallot and sauté, stirring frequently. When fragrant and soft, add the remaining ingredients, stirring well to combine. Reduce the heat to medium-low and simmer for 10 to 15 minutes. Transfer the sauce to the pitcher and blend on ❷ until smooth. Use or cover and store in refrigerator.

✳TIP

Substitute small sweet onions or green onions if you don't have shallots on hand. The onion flavor blends well with the distinctive balsamic vinegar in this special sauce.

YOU'LL NEED:

✓ 72 ounce Pitcher
✓ Blade Assembly
✓ Pitcher Lid

FRESH FIG SAUCE

MAKES ABOUT 1½ CUP

A classic combination, fresh figs and balsamic vinegar, produce an extraordinary topping for grilled meats or sumptuous desserts. There is nothing like fresh figs, but dried figs substitute beautifully if fresh are not available.

10 fresh or dried black mission figs
½ cup balsamic vinegar
⅓ cup white wine
⅓ cup brandy
¼ cup orange juice
¾ cup water
2 tablespoons honey
½ teaspoon ground cardamom (optional)
¼ cup butter

Wash and de-stem the figs if using fresh fruit. Place all of the ingredients, except the butter, into the pitcher and blend on **1** until the sauce is smooth.

In a small sauce pan, melt the butter over medium-low heat. Add the fig sauce from the blender and bring just to a boil. Reduce the heat to low and simmer, stirring frequently, until the sauce thickens, about 20 minutes. Use at once or cover and store in the refrigerator.

✳ TIP

This outrageously wonderful sauce is great when first made when served warm with goat cheese over toasted baguette slices. But, it is even better when stored in the refrigerator for 24 hours and slathered cold over scones or muffins for a special morning treat!

YOU'LL NEED:

✓ 72 ounce Pitcher
✓ Blade Assembly
✓ Pitcher Lid

CRANBERRY & ORANGE RELISH

MAKES ABOUT 4 CUPS

This relish is so delish you will want to use it year around! If fresh cranberries are unavailable, use frozen. For variety, add cinnamon, vanilla or a splash of orange liqueur.

1 medium orange, peeled and pulled into quarters
12 ounce bag fresh cranberries
1 tablespoon sugar, or to taste
1 tablespoon orange liqueur (optional)

Place all ingredients into the pitcher and blend on ❷ until finely chopped and uniform. Taste and add more sugar, if desired. Transfer to a storage bowl, cover and chill for at least two hours, allowing the flavors to marry.

❋TIP

You can only imagine how wonderful this relish tastes when combined with chicken or turkey! Try smoothing this relish on whole wheat bread and adding turkey slices, blue cheese crumbles and arugula for an out-of-this-world sandwich.

YOU'LL NEED:

✓ 72 ounce Pitcher
✓ Blade Assembly
✓ Pitcher Lid

CHOCOLATE CHIP
MINT ICE CREAM
P. 168

CHAPTER NINE

Desserts & Sweet Treats

EASY NEW YORK CHEESECAKE

SERVES 6

Using a few shortcuts, such as a prepared graham cracker crust and your *Ninja™Blender*, makes preparing this cheesecake a breeze.

8 ounces cream cheese, softened
½ cup sugar
2 tablespoons lemon juice
1 teaspoon vanilla extract
pinch salt
2 large eggs
8 inch prepared graham cracker crust

1 cup sour cream
2 tablespoons sugar
½ teaspoon vanilla extract

Place the cream cheese, sugar, lemon juice, extract, salt and eggs in the pitcher and blend on ❷ until smooth. Use a spatula to clean the sides of the pitcher and blend again on ❷ for 30 seconds. Pour the filling into the prepared crust and smooth the top.

Bake at 325°F for 20 minutes. If not set in the center, continue baking for 5-7 minutes or until the center is set. Meanwhile, in a small bowl, combine the sour cream, sugar and vanilla and mix until smooth. Spoon over the top of the cheesecake and continue baking for 10 minutes. Remove from the oven and cool on a wire rack. Refrigerate when cool. Refrigerate any leftovers after serving.

TIP

Top with canned cherries, blueberries or fresh strawberries and cream for the perfect accent to the creamy cheesecake.

YOU'LL NEED:

✓ 72 ounce Pitcher
✓ Blade Assembly
✓ Pitcher Lid

ROCKY ROAD FUDGE PIE

SERVES 8 TO 10

Whip together peanuts, marshmallows and chocolate chips make this a stand-out dessert.

1 cup mini marshmallows
½ cup roasted peanuts
½ cup semi-sweet chocolate chips
16 ounces cream cheese, softened
¼ cup sugar
½ cup lowfat milk
2½ cups prepared whipped cream (or whipped topping)
8-inch prepared chocolate crumb pie crust
½ cup dark fudge sauce

Place the marshmallows, peanuts and chocolate chips in the pitcher and pulse on ❶ to uniformly chop. Remove and place in a large mixing bowl. Place the cream cheese, sugar and milk in the pitcher. Blend on ❷ until very smooth and add the mixture to the chopped marshmallows, peanuts and chips in the mixing bowl. Add the whipped cream and fold in lightly to incorporate. Spoon the pie mixture into the pie crust and smooth evenly over the top.

Freeze for 4 to 6 hours or until set. Before serving, drizzle the dark fudge sauce over the pie. Cut into 8 to 10 pieces and serve right away. Refrigerate or freeze leftovers.

YOU'LL NEED:

✓ 72 ounce Pitcher
✓ Blade Assembly
✓ Pitcher Lid

CHOCOLATE CHIP MINT ICE CREAM

MAKES 3 TO 4 SERVINGS

Peppermint flavor and chocolate chips adorn this rich ice cream. Fill a 1½ to 2 quart ice cream maker for best results.

2½ cups heavy cream

1 cup semi-sweet chocolate chips

2 tablespoons sugar

1 teaspoon peppermint extract

few drops green food coloring, optional

Place the cream, chocolate chips, sugar, peppermint extract and food coloring in the pitcher. Blend on ❷ for about 10 seconds. Pour the ice cream mixture into the freezer bowl or tub of your ice cream maker and proceed as directed.

YOU'LL NEED:

✓ 72 ounce Pitcher

✓ Blade Assembly

✓ Pitcher Lid

PEACHES & CREAM ICE CREAM

MAKES ABOUT 3½ QUARTS

Use ripe peaches for the best flavor and texture and get ready to receive the compliments! This recipe can be used with a 5 or 6 quart ice cream freezer.

5 fresh, ripe peaches, peeled and pitted
6 large eggs
2½ cups sugar, divided
2 tablespoons cornstarch
1 tablespoon vanilla extract
pinch salt
4 cups whole milk
3 cups heavy cream

Place the peaches in the pitcher and blend on ❷ until uniformly smooth. Remove the peaches and chill in the refrigerator.

Clean the pitcher and dry. Place the eggs, sugar, cornstarch, vanilla and salt in the pitcher and blend on ❷ until smooth.

In a large saucepan, heat the milk and cream until steaming. Do not boil. Pour about one-half cup of milk and cream mixture into the egg mixture and blend on ❶ for 10 seconds. Remove the egg mixture from the pitcher and slowly add to the hot milk and cream mixture in the pan, stirring as the two are slowly combined.

Bring the mixture to a very low simmer and stir for about 3 minutes, until smooth and thick. Remove from the heat and chill for several hours.

Just before pouring the cream into the freezer, add the peaches and stir by hand. Pour the ice cream mixture into the freezer and proceed as directed.

YOU'LL NEED:

✓ 72 ounce Pitcher
✓ Blade Assembly
✓ Pitcher Lid

VANILLA BEAN ICE CREAM

MAKES ABOUT 3 QUARTS

Grind whole vanilla beans quickly in your *Ninja™Blender* and add to this ice cream for authentic flavor. This recipe will fill a 5-quart freezer.

4 whole vanilla beans
2½ cups whole milk
2½ cups sugar
½ teaspoon salt
2½ cups light cream
1 tablespoon vanilla extract
5 cups heavy cream

Place the vanilla beans in the pitcher and pulse on ❶ until the beans are fairly ground. Remove the beans and set aside. Clean the blender and dry.

In a large saucepan, scald the whole milk. Remove from the heat and cool. Pour the milk into the pitcher and add the sugar, salt and light cream. Blend on ❷ until very smooth. Pour into a large mixing bowl and add the extract and heavy cream. Stir lightly and add the ground vanilla beans.

Refrigerate the ice cream mixture for 1 hour, then pack and freeze as directed.

YOU'LL NEED:

✓ 72 ounce Pitcher
✓ Blade Assembly
✓ Pitcher Lid

THE KITCHEN®

FROZEN CHOCOLATE FUDGE YOGURT

SERVES 2 TO 3

Perfectly chocolately and smooth – made for two! Use with a 1½ or 2 quart ice cream maker.

¾ cup sugar

2 teaspoons cornstarch

12 ounce can evaporated milk (may substitute lowfat)

1 teaspoon vanilla extract

6 ounces chocolate yogurt

¼ cup chocolate fudge sauce

In a medium saucepan over medium heat, combine the sugar and cornstarch. Stir and add the milk until the mixture begins to steam. Continue cooking and stirring as you add the milk. Continue stirring until the mixture is slightly thickened and smooth. Remove from the heat. Chill for 4 hours in the refrigerator.

Place the vanilla extract and chocolate yogurt in the pitcher and add the fudge sauce. Blend on ❶ until smooth. Slowly pour the cream mixture into the chocolate sauce and blend on ❸ until very smooth.

Pour the chocolate yogurt into an ice cream bowl or tub and freeze as directed.

YOU'LL NEED:

✓ 72 ounce Pitcher

✓ Blade Assembly

✓ Pitcher Lid

RULE THE KITC

LEMON MINT GRANITA

SERVES 4

Very simple and oh, so satisfying on a hot summer day. Using your *Ninja™Blender* eliminates the need to stir the frozen mixture every 30 minutes, making this the easiest dessert of all.

3 large lemons, peeled
4 leaves fresh mint, washed
1 cup water
⅓ superfine sugar (you may also use regular sugar)
mint for garnish, if desired

Place the lemons, mint leaves and water in the pitcher and blend on ❸ until very smooth. Strain all of the juice through a sieve and discard the fruit.

Pour the juice into a bowl or tray. Cover and freeze for 3 to 4 hours, or until almost completely frozen. Remove the ice from the bowl and place in the pitcher. Process on ❸ for 30 seconds, or until the granita is fluffy and uniform. Spoon or pour into 4 small glasses and serve with a spoon at once. Garnish with mint sprigs before serving, if desired.

YOU'LL NEED:

✓ 72 ounce Pitcher
✓ Blade Assembly
✓ Pitcher Lid

WATERMELON GRANITA

SERVES 4 TO 5

Cool, refreshing and a wonderful way to use the ripe watermelon sitting in your refrigerator. You may store the granita for up to 1 month in your freezer before processing in your *Ninja™Blender*. Cover tightly during storage.

6 cups ripe watermelon, peeled and seeded, roughly cut
1 tablespoon lime juice
1½ cups superfine sugar (you may also use regular sugar)

Place the watermelon chunks in the blender in one or two batches, if needed and blend on ❶ for 1 minute. Remove the fruit and strain through a sieve. You should have about 5 cups of juice. Discard the fruit and return the juice to the blender.

Add the lime juice and sugar and blend on ❷ to thoroughly combine the ingredients. Pour the juice into a bowl or ice cube trays and freeze until almost solid, about 3 to 4 hours.

Just before serving, place the iced juice in the blender and process on ❸ for 30 seconds. The granita should be somewhat smooth and a little slushy. Pour into small glasses and serve at once.

YOU'LL NEED:

✓ 72 ounce Pitcher
✓ Blade Assembly
✓ Pitcher Lid

RULE THE KITC

CRISP & RICH BUTTER COOKIES

MAKES ABOUT 6 DOZEN COOKIES

Use a cookie press to create any shapes you want, from bars and stars to hearts and candy canes.

1 cup butter

½ cup sugar

pinch salt

1 large egg

1 teaspoon vanilla extract (substitute lemon extract)

½ teaspoon almond extract

2½ cups all-purpose flour

Place the butter, sugar, salt, egg and extracts in the bowl. Blend on **1** until very light and fluffy. Add the flour and pulse on **1** until combined. Remove the dough paddle and clean the sides of the bowl with a spatula, mixing in any unblended dough. Cover with the lid and chill the dough for about 20 minutes.

Fill a cookie press and press shapes onto ungreased cookie sheets. Bake at 400°F for 8 to 10 minutes. Cookies should be set, but not browned, when done. Cool on wire racks before serving.

✳ TIP

If your cookie dough is too soft to press, pop the dough into the refrigerator to chill for at least 30 minutes. Remove only enough dough to fill the press and keep the remaining amount chilled until filling the press.

YOU'LL NEED:

✓ 40 ounce Bowl

✓ Dough Paddle

✓ Bowl Lid

THE KITCHEN®

CARAMEL OATMEAL BARS

MAKES 14 TO 16 BARS

Filled with gooey caramel, these enticing oat and nut bars will satisfy your craving for chewy and soft, savory and sweet.

⅔ cup butter, softened
1 cup dark brown sugar, packed
1 cup + 3 tablespoons flour
1¼ cups quick-cooking oats
¾ cup walnuts, chopped
12 ounce jar caramel topping (or caramel sauce)

Preheat the oven to 350°F. Grease and flour a 9-inch by 9-inch baking pan.

Place the butter in the bowl and add the sugar. Blend on ❶ until creamy. Add 1 cup of the flour and the oats and pulse on ❶ until well-combined. Use a spatula to clean the sides of the bowl, if needed.

Press one-half of the mixture into the prepared pan and bake for 10 minutes. Remove from the heat and sprinkle with the walnuts. In a small bowl, mix together the caramel and 3 tablespoons flour. Pour over the nuts and top with the remaining oat mixture.

Bake for 20 to 25 minutes and cool on a rack before serving. Refrigerate for about 1 hour before serving to make cutting the bars a little bit easier.

YOU'LL NEED:

✓ 40 ounce Bowl
✓ Dough Paddle
✓ Bowl Lid

RULE THE KITC

ENGLISH TOFFEE COOKIES

MAKES ABOUT 24 COOKIES

Thin and crisp, with a chocolate and almond candy coating!

1 cup butter, softened
½ cup dark brown sugar, packed
½ cup sugar
1 teaspoon vanilla extract
1 egg yolk
2 cups cake flour
pinch salt
10 ounce milk chocolate candy bar, melted
½ cup almonds, chopped

Place the butter, sugars, extract and egg yolk in the bowl and blend on **1** until smooth and creamy. Use a spatula to clean the sides of the bowl. Add 1 cup of flour and salt. Blend on **1** again until smooth. Add the remaining flour and pulse on **1** until smooth.

Spoon the cookie dough onto a baking sheet that has been coated with cooking spray. Allow a 2-inch margin, as the dough will spread.

Lightly spread the chocolate over the dough and sprinkle the nuts over all. Bake at 350°F for 15 to 20 minutes. Cool slightly and cut into small squares. Cool on a wire rack.

YOU'LL NEED:

✓ 40 ounce Bowl
✓ Dough Paddle
✓ Bowl Lid

THE KITCHEN

SOFT MOLASSES DROPS

MAKES ABOUT 3 DOZEN

Full of a warm molasses and sugar flavor with just a hint of ginger and cloves!

¾ cup butter
1 cup dark brown sugar, packed
1 egg
¼ cup dark molasses
2¼ cups flour
2 teaspoons baking soda
¼ teaspoon salt
½ teaspoon cloves
1 teaspoon ground cinnamon
1 teaspoon ground ginger
granulated sugar for garnish

Preheat the oven to 375°F. Place the butter, brown sugar, egg and molasses in the bowl and blend on ❶ until smooth. Place 1 cup of the flour and the remaining ingredients in the bowl and blend on ❶ until well-combined. Clean the sides of the bowl with a spatula as needed. Add the remaining flour and blend again until the flour is incorporated.

Drop the dough by teaspoons onto a baking sheet that has been lightly coated with cooking spray. Sprinkle each cookie with a few drops of water and sprinkle sugar over each cookie. Bake for 10 to 12 minutes, or until set. Cool on a wire rack and store tightly covered.

YOU'LL NEED:

✓ 40 ounce Bowl
✓ Dough Paddle
✓ Bowl Lid

THE KITCHEN®

LEMON, COCONUT & WALNUT BARS

MAKES ABOUT 24 BARS

A wonderful sweet concoction of nutty and tart flavors! Cut these while slightly warm and serve warm or at room temperature. Yum!

½ cup butter
1½ cups dark brown sugar, packed, divided
1 cup all-purpose flour
2 large eggs
2 tablespoons lemon juice
zest 1 lemon
½ teaspoon salt
1 cup shredded coconut
1 cup walnuts, chopped
½ cup raisins

Preheat the oven to 350°F. Place the butter, 1 cup of brown sugar and flour in the bowl and blend on ❶ until crumbly and smooth. Press the mixture evenly into the bottom of an ungreased 9-inch by 13-inch baking pan. Bake for 10 minutes. Remove from the oven and set aside.

Place the remaining brown sugar, eggs, lemon juice, lemon zest and salt in the bowl and blend on ❶ for about 20 seconds. Add the coconut, walnuts and raisins and blend on ❶ for 15 seconds. Pour or spoon the lemon and coconut topping over the flour and butter mixture and spread the topping evenly. Bake for 25 minutes, or until the topping is lightly browned. Cool for 10 minutes and cut into bars.

YOU'LL NEED:

✓ 40 ounce Bowl
✓ Dough Paddle
✓ Bowl Lid

APPLESAUCE CAKE
WITH BUTTERCREAM FROSTING

SERVES 8 TO 10

Packed with juicy apples, nuts and raisins and crowned with fluffy sweet icing, this sublime cake will delight your senses.

2½ cups all-purpose flour
1½ cups sugar
¼ teaspoon baking powder
1½ teaspoons baking soda
1½ teaspoons salt
1 teaspoon ground cinnamon
½ teaspoon ground cloves
½ teaspoon ground allspice
½ cup shortening
½ cup water
1½ cups unsweetened applesauce
2 medium eggs
½ cup walnuts, chopped
1 cup raisins

Buttercream Frosting
¼ cup butter, softened
1¼ cups powdered sugar
½ teaspoon vanilla extract
pinch salt
2 teaspoons milk

Preheat the oven to 350°F. Grease and flour a 9-inch by 13-inch baking pan. Place the flour, sugar, baking powder, soda, salt, and spices in the pitcher and pulse on ❶ for 10 seconds. Add the shortening, water, applesauce and eggs and blend again on ❶ until smooth. Use a spatula to clean the sides of the pitcher if needed. Add the nuts and raisins and pulse on ❶, just until the walnuts and raisins are incorporated.

Pour the batter into the prepared pan. Bake for 50 to 60 minutes or until the center is firm. Remove and cool on a rack.

To prepare the frosting, place the butter, sugar, vanilla, salt and milk in the pitcher and blend on ❸ until the frosting is very smooth and fluffy. Frost the cooled cake and serve.

YOU'LL NEED:

✓ 72 ounce Pitcher
✓ Blade Assembly
✓ Pitcher Lid

THE KITCHEN

PINEAPPLE NUT CRUMB CAKE

SERVES 8 TO 10

This moist and delectable cake offers a twist on traditional pineapple upside-down cake. Pineapple slices and a rich crumbly cake take the top!

½ cup butter
¾ cup sugar
2 eggs
1½ teaspoons vanilla extract
1¼ cups all-purpose flour
1 teaspoon baking powder
1 fresh pineapple, peeled, cored, quartered lengthwise and sliced

Crumb Topping
1¼ cups all-purpose flour
½ cup sugar
¼ teaspoon ground cinnamon
½ cup butter
½ cup walnuts

Preheat the oven to 350°F. Butter the bottom and sides of a 10-inch springform pan. Place the butter in the bowl and blend on ❶ until very fluffy. Add the sugar and blend again on ❶ for 10 seconds. Use a spatula to clean the sides of the bowl. Add the eggs and vanilla and blend on ❶ until uniformly smooth.

Add the flour and baking powder and blend on ❶ just until all the ingredients are moistened. Pour the batter into the prepared pan.

In the bowl, combine the flour, sugar and cinnamon for the crumb topping. Add the butter and walnuts and pulse on ❶ for 20 seconds. Remove and set aside.

Place the pineapple slices on top of the batter, leaving a ½-inch margin around the outside edge. Scatter the crumb mixture over the top. Bake for 50 to 60 minutes, or until the cake is firm.

Remove the cake and cool. Remove the pan rim and place on a serving platter.

YOU'LL NEED:

✓ 40 ounce Bowl
✓ Dough Paddle
✓ Bowl Lid

RULE THE KITC

KEY LIME PIE

SERVES 6 TO 8

Love the smooth and tart flavor of bright Key limes?
This is your dessert!

2 large eggs
14 ounce can sweetened condensed milk
4 key limes, juiced to equal ½ cup (you may also use
the juice of limes or bottled lime juice)
1 8-inch prepared graham cracker crust
1 cup whipped cream

Preheat the oven to 350°F. Whip the eggs on **3** until light and frothy, add the milk and lime juice and blend on **2** to incorporate.

Pour the batter into the graham cracker crust and bake for 10 minutes. Remove and cool. Chill for about 2 hours before serving. Serve with whipped cream.

✳ TIP

What makes key limes so special? Typical limes, or Persian limes, have a tart, yet somewhat smooth flavor. Key limes are much smaller and have a higher acidic acid and mouth-puckering tartness. As such, key limes are prized in sauces, marinades and, of course, key lime pie. If you can't find key limes in your grocery store, you may be able to find bottled key lime juice, or simply substitute Persian limes in equal proportions.

YOU'LL NEED:

✓ Pitcher
✓ Blade Assembly
✓ Pitcher Lid

THE KITCHEN®

CHAPTER TEN

Condiments
& Spice Blends

LEMON & GARLIC AIOLI

MAKES ABOUT 1½ CUPS

Homemade spreads, such as aioli or mayonnaise, really need to be given time during blending to fully incorporate the oil into the eggs. Try starting by adding oil in drops and then pour using a very thin stream of oil. This is one recipe that shouldn't be rushed because the end results are so delicious. Please note that this aioli contains raw eggs.

4 egg yolks
2 cloves garlic
¾ cup canola oil
juice 1 lemon (3- 4 tablespoons)
pinch salt
pinch white or black pepper

Place the yolks in the bowl and add the garlic. Blend on ❷ until smooth. With the blender running on ❷, slowly add a few drops of oil to the egg/garlic mixture through the pour tab opening in the lid. Wait for the yolks to absorb the oil and then add a thin stream of oil into the egg/garlic mixture as the blender continues to run. If the mixture gets too thick, add a few drops of water or oil to thin. Spoon the aioli into a bowl and gently fold in the lemon salt and pepper. Adjust the seasonings to taste.

Store the aioli in the refrigerator for up to 1 week.

✳TIP

Use this rich, garlicky sauce in hearty sandwiches. Start with dark rye bread, spread with aioli, then add thin slices of black forest ham, Swiss cheese, thin shavings of purple onion, tomato and romaine lettuce. Add another thin layer of aioli on top and grab plenty of napkins!

YOU'LL NEED:

✓ 40 ounce Bowl
✓ Blade Assembly
✓ Bowl Lid

RICH & CREAMY MAYONNAISE

MAKES ABOUT 1½ CUPS MAYONNAISE

If you've never had homemade mayonnaise, you'll be surprised by the delicate flavor and richness of this spread. Try to save some for everyone else! Please note that this dressing contains raw eggs.

2 egg yolks
pinch salt
¼ teaspoon sugar
½ teaspoon dry mustard
1½ cups canola oil
¼ cup white vinegar
cayenne pepper, optional

Place the yolks in the pitcher and add the salt, sugar and mustard. Blend on ❷ until smooth. Open the lid pour tab and add a few drops of the oil as the blender continues to run and, as the egg yolks absorb the oil, continue blending and adding the oil in a very thin stream. Add drops of water as needed to thin the mixture. After blending the oil into the yolks, add the vinegar and cayenne pepper to taste, if desired. Blend on ❶ for just a few seconds to incorporate.

Store the mayonnaise in the refrigerator for up to 1 week.

YOU'LL NEED:

✓ 72 ounce Pitcher
✓ Blade Assembly
✓ Pitcher Lid

RULE THE KITC

CRUNCHY THAI PEANUT SPREAD

MAKES ABOUT 1 CUP

A perfect accompaniment to chicken satay, pad Thai or any Asian beef dish. The peanuts should be chunky, not smooth, for best results.

2 cups roasted peanuts (salted or unsalted)
3 tablespoons canola oil
3 to 4 tablespoons soy sauce

Place the peanuts in the pitcher and pulse on ❶ until uniformly chunky. Use a spatula to clean the sides of the pitcher. Add the canola oil and soy sauce and continue pulsing for 30 seconds. Store for up to 2 weeks in the refrigerator.

✳TIP

All too often peanut sauce is thin and watery. Not so with this crunchy blend! Use it in place of peanut butter in your favorite dishes and enjoy the soy sauce twist.

THE KITCHEN®

YOU'LL NEED:

✓ 72 ounce Pitcher
✓ Blade Assembly
✓ Pitcher Lid

HERBS DE PROVENCE MIX

MAKES ABOUT 1½ CUPS

Sprinkle this mix over salads, pasta or broiled steaks for a spark of flavor.

1 bunch fresh sage leaves
1 bunch fresh thyme leaves
1 sprig fresh rosemary
½ bulb fennel, cleaned
¼ teaspoon coarse salt
¼ teaspoon freshly ground black pepper

Place all ingredients into the pitcher and blend on ❶ until uniformly chopped and finely mixed. Store in the refrigerator in a glass jar, freeze, or use right away.

✳TIP

This classic mix of herbs is perfectly balanced and, when using fresh herbs instead of dried, the flavors mingle and become more intense with time.

YOU'LL NEED:

✓ 72 ounce Pitcher
✓ Blade Assembly
✓ Pitcher Lid

ASIAN GINGER SPICE BLEND

MAKES ABOUT 1 CUP

Fresh ginger contributes a powerful punch of flavor to this fresh mix. Use with chicken or fish for best results.

1-inch piece fresh ginger, peeled
¼ cup onion powder
¼ cup garlic salt
¼ cup black pepper
2 tablespoons red pepper flakes

Place all of the ingredients in the pitcher and blend on ❶ for 15 seconds, or until the ginger is completely incorporated with the remaining ingredients. Store in a tightly sealed container and refrigerate.

✳TIP

Change up this blend by including lemon pepper, or five spice powder in place of the onion powder. Try adding ¼ cup of olive oil to create a super fish rub prior to grilling.

YOU'LL NEED:

✓ 72 ounce Pitcher
✓ Blade Assembly
✓ Pitcher Lid

RULE THE KITC

ITALIAN SEASONING MIX

MAKES ½ CUP SEASONING

A classic, flavorful blend of savory herbs and spices. Store this herb blend in the refrigerator in a tightly sealed container.

¼ cup fresh marjoram leaves
1 tablespoon fresh sage leaves
2 tablespoons fresh rosemary
2 tablespoons fresh oregano leaves
2 tablespoons fresh basil leaves
2 tablespoons fresh thyme
2 tablespoons fresh savory (optional)
1 tablespoon black pepper
2 cloves garlic, peeled (or you may use 2 tablespoons garlic salt)

Place all ingredients in the pitcher and blend on **1** until uniform. Use as a rub for beef, or pat on chicken prior to grilling. Store in a tightly sealed container in the refrigerator.

TIP

This mix will make enough rub for 2 large steaks or several chicken breasts.

YOU'LL NEED:

✓ 72 ounce Pitcher
✓ Blade Assembly
✓ Pitcher Lid

FRESH HOT DOG & HAMBURGER RELISH

MAKES ABOUT 1 CUP OF RELISH

Take me out to the ballgame with this spicy, sweet and crunchy spread!

1 large white onion, peeled and quartered
1 rib celery
8 sweet pickles or gherkins
1 green bell pepper, cored and seeded, cut in quarters
2 cloves garlic, peeled
¼ cup canned tomato paste
¼ cup cider vinegar
1½ tablespoons chili powder
2 tablespoons dark brown sugar
1 teaspoon Dijon mustard

Place the onion, celery, pickles, pepper and garlic in the pitcher. Pulse on ❶ until uniformly chopped. The mixture should not be smooth. Add the tomato paste, vinegar, and remaining ingredients. Blend again on ❶ until uniform. Spoon the relish into a glass or plastic container and cover tightly. Store for up to 2 weeks in the refrigerator.

✳TIP

Go beyond hamburgers and hot dogs! Pack this relish on top of baked potatoes, toss onto salads, pair up with crackers and cheese, or spread on lunchbox sandwiches in place of mayo or mustard.

YOU'LL NEED:

✓ 72 ounce Pitcher
✓ Blade Assembly
✓ Pitcher Lid

RULE THE KITC

SMOKED HAM & ONION SPREAD

MAKES APPROXIMATELY 3 CUPS

Cover thick slices of dark rye bread or whole grain crackers with this smoky spread and enjoy the resulting feast!

3 cups smoked ham, cut in large pieces
¼ small white onion, peeled
1 large egg, hard-cooked and peeled
¼ cup Fresh Hot Dog & Hamburger Relish (see p. 193)
1 cup regular or lowfat mayonnaise
1 tablespoon prepared Dijon mustard

Place the ham pieces and onion into the pitcher and blend on ❶ until evenly chopped. Add the egg, relish, mayonnaise and mustard and pulse on ❶ until uniform, but not completely smooth. Spoon the spread into a glass or plastic container and cover tightly. Store in the refrigerator. Keeps for up to 1 week.

✳ TIP

This is a perfect party spread for hungry guests. Make it even more special by spreading it on buttered baguette slices, topping each slice with shredded Swiss cheese and broiling until the cheese is melted and warm.

YOU'LL NEED:

✓ 72 ounce Pitcher
✓ Blade Assembly
✓ Pitcher Lid

ROASTED GARLIC BUTTER

MAKES ½ POUND FLAVORED BUTTER

A really good garlic butter will stand up to a hearty grilled beef steak (a pat of garlic butter on a grilled steak goes a long way), a layered sandwich and even a smidgen in with your breakfast omelette. This butter takes a bit of time, but achieves all that a marvelous and flavorful spread should be. Don't be shy – enjoy that garlic!

3 heads garlic, tops cut off to expose the individual cloves
3 tablespoons extra virgin olive oil
½ pound butter, softened
1 sprig fresh parsley

Preheat the oven to 400°F. Peel off the outer layers of the heads of garlic, leaving just a few layers to hold the cloves. Place the garlic heads in a baking pan and drizzle with the olive oil. Cover with foil and bake for 30 to 35 minutes, or until the garlic cloves are very soft and respond to pressure from your fingers.

Remove the garlic from the oven and set aside to cool. When cool, squeeze the garlic cloves out of each head and remove the garlic from the cloves. Place the garlic in the pitcher. Add the butter and parsley to the garlic and blend on ❶ until smooth. Use a spatula to clean the sides of the pitcher and blend again on ❶ for 20 seconds.

Place a large square of foil on a counter and spoon the garlic butter onto the foil. With your hands or two spoons shape a rounded log of butter on the foil, then roll the foil around the butter until it is sealed, with the ends tucked in.

Refrigerate for at least 4 hours before using. To serve, use a sharp knife to cut a sliver from the butter as needed. Refrigerate until use.

YOU'LL NEED:

✓ 72 ounce Pitcher
✓ Blade Assembly
✓ Pitcher Lid

SWEET ORANGE BUTTER

MAKES ½ POUND FLAVORED BUTTER

The perfect butter to accompany a hot sweet muffin!

½ cup dried cranberries
½ pound butter, softened
1 teaspoon orange juice
1 tablespoon orange zest
¼ cup powdered sugar

Place the dried cranberries in the pitcher and blend on ❷ until the berries are mashed together. Add the remaining ingredients and blend on ❶ until uniform. Use a spatula to clean the sides of the pitcher and blend again, if needed.

Place a large square of foil over a small decorative bowl and press it so that the foil takes on the shape of the bowl. Spoon the butter into the foil-lined bowl and press so that the butter takes the shape of the bowl. Chill for at least 6 hours. When ready to use, remove the foil and butter from the bowl, remove the foil from the butter and invert the butter onto a small serving plate. Serve at once.

YOU'LL NEED:

✓ 72 ounce Pitcher
✓ Blade Assembly
✓ Pitcher Lid

CREAMY HORSERADISH SPREAD

MAKES 1 CUP SPREAD

Sharp, piquant horseradish is often overlooked because it can be so over-powering, however it really deserves a spread of its own. Use sparingly with prime rib or any other cut of beef and, as your taste adapts, become a little daring and add more.

3 tablespoons white horseradish (not cream)
½ cup sour cream
½ cup mayonnaise
pinch salt
pinch black pepper
½ sprig fresh parsley

Place all of the ingredients in the bowl and blend on ❸ until smooth. Use a spatula to clean the sides of the pitcher, if needed.

Chill for at least 2 hours before using. Store in a tightly closed container for up to 1 week.

✳TIP

A whole horseradish root doesn't really have much flavor, but cutting into it brings out enzymes that pack a wallop! This spread softens the sharp flavor by combining it with mayonnaise. Substitute sour cream or plain yogurt and add a handful of herbs for a great flavor change.

YOU'LL NEED:

✓ 40 ounce Bowl
✓ Blade Assembly
✓ Bowl Lid

RULE THE KITC

MAPLE
CINNAMON
PEACHES & PLUMS
P. 206

CHAPTER ELEVEN

Baby & Toddler Treats

BAKED CRISPY MOZZARELLA STICKS

MAKES 8 CHEESE STICKS

Who can resist crunchy cheese sticks? Boost this already healthy dish by using whole wheat bread and adding wheat germ to the bread crumb mixture.

4 slices stale or day old bread
½ cup Parmesan cheese, finely grated
½ teaspoon dried basil
½ teaspoon dried parsley
2 eggs
4 tablespoons milk
8 sticks string cheese
olive or canola oil cooking spray

Place the bread into the pitcher and blend on ② into medium crumbs. Add the Parmesan cheese, basil and parsley and blend until crumbs are fine. Transfer the bread crumb mixture to a shallow dish. Beat the eggs and milk together in a shallow bowl.

Dip each cheese stick into the egg mixture, coating well, then roll in the bread crumbs. Re-dip in the egg mixture and roll again in the bread crumbs to form a thick crust. Repeat with each cheese stick. Place the cheese sticks on a baking sheet, cover and refrigerate for 30 to 40 minutes.

Preheat the oven to 350°F degrees. Spray the cheese sticks with olive or canola oil and bake for 6 to 8 minutes. Watch closely to remove the sticks before the cheese melts. Serve cooled.

YOU'LL NEED:

✓ **72 ounce Pitcher**
✓ **Blade Assembly**
✓ **Pitcher Lid**

HEALTHY MAC & CHEESE

MAKES 8 TO 10 SERVINGS

Pureed carrots add vitamins and color to a classic kid-favorite!

2 slices stale or day old bread
1 medium carrot, peeled, and steamed
½ cup whole milk
1 cup cottage cheese
8 ounces elbow macaroni, uncooked
1½ cups cheddar cheese, grated
2 tablespoons unsalted butter

Place the bread in the pitcher and blend on ② into fine crumbs. Remove the bread crumbs to a small bowl. Place the cooked carrot and milk in the blender and blend on ② until the carrot is pureed, cleaning the sides of the pitcher with a spatula as needed. Add the cottage cheese and pulse until just blended.

Prepare the elbow macaroni according to the package directions. When the pasta is done, drain in a colander and transfer to a 9-inch by x 13-inch baking dish. Add the blended carrot mixture and cheese and stir until the ingredients are well combined.

Preheat the oven to 350°F degrees. Melt the butter in a small saucepan over low heat or in microwave. Toss the bread crumbs with the melted butter and scatter over the top of macaroni. Bake for 30 to 40 minutes, or until top is golden brown and casserole is hot and melty. Cool slightly and serve.

YOU'LL NEED:

✓ 72 ounce Pitcher
✓ Blade Assembly
✓ Pitcher Lid

RULE THE KITCHE

BANANA RICE PUDDING

MAKES ABOUT 2 CUPS, ENOUGH FOR 4 TO 6 TODDLER SERVINGS

A tasty and nourishing treat. Rice milk may be substituted for cow's milk if your child has an intolerance to dairy foods.

1 ripe banana, peeled
1 cup cooked brown rice
¼ cup warmed milk (more may be needed)
⅛ teaspoon pure vanilla extract
⅛ teaspoon ground cinnamon

Place all ingredients into the pitcher and blend on ② until the consistency is appropriate for your child. Use a spatula to clean the sides of the blender as necessary. If the pudding is too thick, add additional milk. Serve right away or cover and store in refrigerator.

TIP

Even little ones appreciate the great spice flavors of vanilla and cinnamon. Serve warmed with a little bit of butter for a special treat.

YOU'LL NEED:

✓ **72 ounce Pitcher**
✓ **Blade Assembly**
✓ **Pitcher Lid**

SMOOTH BAKED APPLE

MAKES ABOUT 1 CUP, ENOUGH FOR 2 TO 3 TODDLER SERVINGS

Sweeter apples work best for this dish, as apples such as Granny Smith may be too tart for your baby.

1 medium apple, cored
½ teaspoon pure maple syrup
1 whole cinnamon stick (or ½ teaspoon ground cinnamon)
1 tablespoon ricotta cheese

Preheat the oven to 350°F. Place the apple on a large piece of foil. Drizzle maple syrup over the top and into the core of apple. Place the cinnamon stick into core. Loosely wrap foil up around apple, twisting at the top to seal and place on a baking dish. Bake for 35 to 40 minutes, until the apple is very soft.

Remove the apple from the oven, discard the cinnamon stick and while still warm, but cool enough to handle, peel the apple if desired. Place into the pitcher and blend on ❶ until the apple is almost pureed. Add the ricotta cheese to the apple and pulse to combine. Serve warm or cover and store in refrigerator until use.

YOU'LL NEED:

√ 72 ounce Pitcher
√ Blade Assembly
√ Pitcher Lid

RULE THE KITCHE

PARSNIPS, POTATO AND PEARS, OH MY

MAKES ABOUT 2 CUPS, ENOUGH FOR 6 TO 8 TODDLER MEALS

The pears add a lovely sweetness to this nutrient packed trio.

1 medium garnet yam or sweet potato, peeled, halved lengthwise and thickly sliced
1 medium parsnip peeled, halved lengthwise and thickly sliced
1 small pear, peeled, cored and chopped
pinch ground nutmeg
pinch ground cinnamon

In a medium saucepan, place the yam and parsnip in about 2 cups of water and bring to a boil over medium-high heat. Reduce the heat, cover and simmer until the vegetables are almost softened. Add the pear and continue cooking until tender, about 6 minutes.

Drain, reserving the cooking water and transfer the cooked fruit and vegetables into the pitcher, along with the nutmeg and cinnamon. Blend on ② until the mixture is pureed and smooth. Add some of the reserved cooking water if a thinner consistency is desired. Serve warm or cover and store in refrigerator.

YOU'LL NEED:

✓ 72 ounce Pitcher
✓ Blade Assembly
✓ Pitcher Lid

PERFECTLY PEACHY CHICKEN

MAKES 2 TO 3 CUPS, ENOUGH FOR 8 TO 10 BABY/TODDLER SERVINGS

This complete healthy meal is a sweet way to get protein into your little ones.

1 small boneless, skinless chicken breast, cut into 1 inch pieces
1 small sweet potato or garnet yam, peeled, and cut into 1 inch pieces
1 to 1½ cups apple juice
½ fresh peach, peeled, pitted and chopped

Place the chicken and potato in a small saucepan and add enough apple juice to cover. Bring just to a boil over medium-high heat, reduce to medium-low and simmer until almost tender. Add the peach and continue cooking until tender, about 4 to 6 minutes.

Drain off any remaining apple juice and reserve. Place the cooked chicken, potato and peach into the pitcher and blend on **2** until pureed, adding some of the reserved apple juice to obtain your desired consistency. Use immediately or cover and store in the refrigerator, reheating before serving.

YOU'LL NEED:

✓ 72 ounce Pitcher
✓ Blade Assembly
✓ Pitcher Lid

RULE THE KITCHE

MAPLE CINNAMON PEACHES & PLUMS

MAKES ABOUT 2 CUPS, ENOUGH FOR 6 TO 8 BABY/TODDLER SERVINGS

This yummy healthy dessert is sweet without the addition of sugar.

1 large ripe peach, peeled, halved and pitted
2 fresh ripe plums, quartered
1 cup plain yogurt
1 teaspoon pure maple syrup
pinch ground cinnamon

Place the peach and plums into the bowl and blend on ❶ until pureed. Add the yogurt, maple syrup and cinnamon, mixing on ❶ to blend. Serve or cover and store in the refrigerator. Makes about 2 cups, enough for 6 to 8 baby/toddler servings.

✳TIP

Puree the peach and plums in your *Ninja*™ *blender* until very smooth and use this peachy plum dessert within a few days while fresh. This recipe does not freeze well, but can be stored in the refrigerator for up to 2 days.

YOU'LL NEED:

✓ **40 ounce Bowl**
✓ **Blade Assembly**
✓ **Blade Lid**

CHEESE & AVOCADO QUESADILLAS

MAKES 2 TO 4 SERVINGS TODDLER SERVINGS

Mixing the butternut puree with the cheese is a great way to get your toddlers to eat their vegetables.

1 small butternut squash, halved and seeded
½ cup canned pinto beans, drained
1 avocado, peeled, pitted and chopped
½ cup cheddar cheese, shredded
4 whole wheat tortillas
olive oil cooking spray

Preheat the oven to 400°F degrees. Place the butternut squash on a baking sheet, flesh side down and bake for 45 to 50 minutes. When cool enough to handle, scoop out the flesh and transfer to the pitcher. Blend on ② until the squash is pureed, about 2 minutes. Measure about ½ cup of the puree for the recipe and store the remaining puree, covered, in the refrigerator for another use. Clean the blender and dry.

Spray the underside of 2 tortillas with olive oil cooking spray and place on a baking sheet. Place the beans and avocado in the pitcher and blend on ② until smooth. Spread the mixture over the 2 tortillas. Combine the butternut squash puree with the cheddar cheese and crumble over the beans.

Place the 2 remaining tortillas on top and spray with the olive oil. Bake for 5 or 6 minutes, or until the cheese melts and the outside of the tortillas are crisp. Serve with a mild salsa, if desired.

YOU'LL NEED:

✓ 72 ounce Pitcher
✓ Blade Assembly
✓ Pitcher Lid

RULE THE KITCHE

GREEN BEANS WITH ROASTED RED BELL PEPPER DIP

MAKES 2 TO 4 SERVINGS

The roasted red pepper puree makes a sweet nutritious dip and the green beans are easy for little hands to grip!

1 large red bell pepper, washed
20 fresh green beans, washed and strings removed

Using tongs, hold the red bell pepper over the flame of a gas burner or place under the broiler in the oven. Turn frequently to blacken on all sides. Place the pepper into a paper bag and let sit for 10 to 12 minutes. Remove the pepper from bag and easily slip off the outer skin. Cut the pepper in half and remove the seeds.

Place the roasted, seeded pepper into the pitcher and blend on ❷ until pureed and very smooth.

Steam the green beans until just tender. Cool and serve to your toddler with roasted red bell pepper puree for dipping.

YOU'LL NEED:

✓ **72 ounce Pitcher**
✓ **Blade Assembly**
✓ **Pitcher Lid**

GOLDEN MASHED POTATO PUFFS

MAKES ABOUT 24 PUFFS

Cheesy, warm and wonderful, these puffs will get the attention of kids and adults alike!

4 medium russet potatoes, peeled and diced
½ cup milk, warmed
1 egg, beaten
½ teaspoon baking powder
2 teaspoons white flour
½ cup Parmesan cheese, grated
½ teaspoon salt

In a large saucepan filled with water, bring the potatoes to a boil, and then reduce the heat to medium-low and simmer until tender. Drain the potatoes and place into the pitcher. Add the remaining ingredients, reserving 2 tablespoons of Parmesan cheese, and pulse on ❶ until blended.

Preheat the oven to 350°F degrees. Drop the potato mixture by teaspoons onto a non-stick baking sheet. Sprinkle the potato puffs with the remaining Parmesan cheese and bake for 20 minutes. Allow the puffs to cool slightly and serve warm.

YOU'LL NEED:

✓ **72 ounce Pitcher**
✓ **Blade Assembly**
✓ **Pitcher Lid**

RULE THE KITCHE

INDEX